How To Get Paid $73,150.00 For <u>Only</u> Mailing 1,000 Letters!

A Revolutionary New Way To Stay Home And Get Rich In The Booming Direct-Mail Industry.

Because this information is somewhat controversial, it is URGENT that you read and understand the IMPORTANT LEGAL DISCLAIMER in the beginning of this book. Please do this first. *Thank you.*

This book is dedicated to Russ von Hoelscher, the man who made my wife, Eileen, and I millions of dollars when we were first getting started.

Russ is also the marketing expert who discovered the basic wealth-making secret behind this all new way to get paid up to $73,150.00 for mailing 1,000 letters.

Thank you, Russ!

Important Legal Disclaimer
(Please read first.)

This book is published for informational purposes only and is based solely on our knowledge, experience, and educated opinions. It tells you about our all new Direct-Mail secret that has the potential power to let you get paid as much as $73,150.00 for only mailing 1,000 letters. However, there are absolutely NO GUARANTEES and/or NO PROMISES being made that you (or any reader of this book) 'will' earn $73,150.00 or any specific sum of money with the information we will freely share with you. **You must understand this before you read another word.** We do not promise or guarantee, in any way, shape, or form, that you will make any specific sum of money with this new discovery. IT IS URGENT THAT YOU KNOW THIS. Also, this book is not intended to persuade you to become an Affiliate Mailer for our new 'Mailing Co-Op Wealth System.' The specific information about this new 3-level Affiliate Mailing Program is given to you in an attempt to prove to you that it is potentially possible to get paid up to $73,150.00 for mailing only 1,000 Direct-Mail letters. Again, this is based on the best-of-the-best of all of our knowledge, experience, and research; so telling you about our specific Program is the best way we can help you understand why it is potentially possible to earn huge sums of money for only mailing a small number of Direct-Mail letters. However, because this book is sold for informational purposes only, we have written a complete Chapter that shows you the basic steps necessary to develop your own Affiliate Mailing Program, just like ours, to use the information in the fullest way. Also, all income figures and charts in this book are used as mathematical income projections only and not as a promise or guarantee that you will earn these specific sums of money or achieve the percentages of response that we base our income projections on. Do you understand all of this? If not, keep reading this legal disclaimer until you do. **Once you DO understand everything I have just said, you must also know that WE FIRMLY BELIEVE that this is the single greatest**

discovery for the average person to get rich with Direct-Mail Marketing! This is only our strong belief and opinion, but as you'll see, Direct-Mail is a proven way to get rich. However, because of many problems, it is getting harder and harder for the average person to make money with Direct-Mail. We have been searching for many years for the most powerful way to help people get rich with Direct-Mail. After all, this is a marketing method that has brought our company many millions of dollars, so we know that it works. However, <u>because</u> <u>of</u> <u>all</u> <u>the</u> <u>problems</u> <u>associated</u> <u>with</u> <u>Direct-Mail,</u> <u>it</u> <u>has</u> <u>been</u> <u>VERY</u> <u>FRUSTRATING</u> <u>for</u> <u>us</u> <u>to</u> <u>be</u> <u>able</u> <u>to</u> <u>help</u> <u>average</u> <u>people</u> <u>cash</u> <u>in</u> <u>from</u> <u>this</u> <u>multi-billion</u> <u>dollar</u> <u>marketing</u> <u>method</u>. *<u>UNTIL</u> <u>NOW</u>!!!* Please read this book and find out EXACTLY why we firmly believe this is the ultimate way for average people to get rich in the booming Direct-Mail industry. With all of this in mind, especially the things I told you about in the beginning of this legal disclaimer, let's begin...

TABLE OF CONTENTS

INTRODUCTION

Can you really make $73,150.00 for only mailing 1000 letters? The answer is "YES!" This book will prove it to you!

By T.J. Rohleder

This small book tells you about a new — but ROCK SOLID WAY to stay home and make huge sums of money from the comfort, privacy, and security of your own home.

Be prepared to be shocked and amazed!

As you will see, everything between the covers of this book is true! Our new 'Mailing Co-Op Wealth System' is an all new way to cash in on the power of Direct-Mail Marketing. It's like no other money-making plan or program you have ever seen!

How To Get The Most Value From This Small Book

The majority of this book contains the printed transcript of a 70-minute audio presentation that was given by myself and Chris Lakey. We delivered this presentation to a group of our best Clients — to tell them about our amazing new 3-level Affiliate Mailing Program that makes it possible to get paid up to $73,150.00 or more — for mailing as few as 1,000 Direct-Mail letters. **We wanted**

---

you to have these slightly edited transcripts so you could get all of the basic secrets behind this simple business plan as we first introduced them to our Clients.

Reading a printed transcript of an audio presentation can be difficult. So I have made some key sentences a bold typeface and written some dialog throughout these transcripts, to help you gain a better understanding of this information. **PLUS, to make it even easier for you to read these transcripts, you can go to the special Web-Site that's listed on the bottom of each right-hand page and play the actual 70-minute recording of our presentation!** You must try this!

There is no better way to fully understand something than to be able to read and listen at the same time. The Internet makes this so easy to do. Just go to our Web-Site, hit the 'play' button, and listen as you read. This lets you get through the book faster and helps you gain a better understanding of the powerful money-making ideas we are sharing with you. As you'll see, we make it so easy for you to listen to the entire presentation. You can listen to the presentation in one 70-minute sitting, or start and stop the recording at your convenience as you read along and study my additional comments. Please try this! Go to our Web-Site RIGHT NOW and listen as you read.

Going to our Web-Site and listening to our presentation as you read lets you gain the fullest understanding of how simple and easy this new business plan is. Do this and you will be shocked and amazed! As you will see and hear, this really does give you the potential power to get paid huge sums of money for only mailing a small number of Direct-Mail letters!

How We Stumbled Onto This
Amazing Direct-Mail Secret

I wish I could take credit for this new way to get paid up to $73,150.00 for mailing 1,000 letters. Unfortunately, I can't.

This initial discovery was made by my dear friend and mentor: <u>Russ von Hoelscher</u>.

Russ is a marketing genius who helped my wife, Eileen, and I make millions of dollars when we were first getting started back in the late 1980's.

We had just started our Mail-Order business when we first met Russ and we were making pretty good money by running small ads in a handful of national magazines. Russ saw our small ads, liked the idea behind the product we were selling, and sent us a brochure for his consulting services. He included a small note that simply said: *"I have seen your ad and your product, and like what you're doing. I think I can help you. Please give me a call."*

So we called him and our lives were instantly changed.

Russ von Hoelscher went to work to help us take the product that we were already selling through small display ads and multiply it through other media. He introduced us to several of his key contacts and told us what to do and how to do it. We listened very carefully to all of his powerful advice and, to make a long story short, we brought in millions of dollars within a few short years!

Yes, that's the power of working closely with a marketing genius like Russ von Hoelscher and then doing everything he tells you to do!

We were already bringing in around $16,000.00 a month when Russ first sent us the letter that told us he could help us. That was a lot of money to us at the time because we had struggled financially for so many years. **It also meant that we already had a nice foundation underneath us when Russ began helping us...** After all — it was the small display ads for our first product (called *'Dialing for Dollars'*) that first attracted Russ to us... This made it easier for him to use his two decades of knowledge and experience to help us turn our initial income into...

Almost $100,000.00 a week...
in just 9 months!

Yes, thanks to the amazing power of leverage, Russ was able to help us go from sixteen thousands dollars a month to almost $100,000.00 a week in the first nine months! He helped us create a huge explosion of wealth! By the time the smoke cleared — we had brought in over ten million dollars in <u>less</u> than 5 years. Our lives were instantly transformed! Suddenly we knew all of the secrets to making millions of dollars — and we have <u>never</u> looked back.

Since that time we have brought in tens of millions of dollars: a grand total of over 100 million dollars in sales in our first 19 years. And it would not have been made without all of the initial help, support, and guidance that was given to us by Russ von Hoelscher.

Our rags to riches story is now a legend with all of our own Clients who we have strived to help... Throughout the years we have held hundreds of seminars, workshops, and tele-seminars where we freely shared the story of how Russ von Hoelscher took us by the hand and helped us bring in over ten million dollars in our first four years.

Needless to say, Russ has become somewhat of a celebrity in our circle of influences and with the thousands of Clients of our companies.

Many people have been greatly inspired by the fact that my wife, Eileen, and I struggled financially for so many years before we first stumbled onto our small success that first attracted Russ von Hoelscher to us... They get to know us and realize that we are the most average people in the world and they walk away from our seminars and workshops knowing that if people like us can make millions of dollars — then they can do it, too... And they're right! They really can do it. You see — once they come to our seminars

— and spend a couple of days with us — they realize that it is the marketing methods and strategies that Russ first taught us that caused over ten million dollars to come pouring in to us and that it had nothing to do with 'luck'... Once they know this — their entire lives are changed forever! They are no longer the same because now they realize that:

The same marketing methods
that have made us millions of dollars
can make <u>them</u> a huge fortune, too!

And they're right!

They really can!

Once people realize that it's the marketing methods that can make them rich — they are in the powerful position to make their own fortune! Now they start developing a hunger for learning the best marketing methods that <u>they</u> can use to make their own fortune. They start asking better questions and getting better answers. They begin to see possibilities where none existed before. Now they start looking for the <u>best</u> strategies, methods, and formulas that are making a fortune for other people. So they can find a way to apply them in their own lives.

This new level of thinking causes them to ask questions such as, *"What is the greatest wealth making secret you have ever discovered?"* Or *"What is the one thing that Russ von Hoelscher did for you that made you more money then anything else?"* The answer to BOTH of these questions is the same: <u>Direct-Mail</u>.

Direct-Mail is the #1 secret
that made us millions of dollars
in no time flat! It can quickly
make <u>you</u> millions of dollars, too!

Direct-Mail is a powerful marketing method that is collectively

---

bringing in well over a billion dollars a day to all of the individuals and companies who are using it. It is the world's most powerful way to sell someone a product or service. Yes, when done correctly — Direct-Mail is the world's most powerful method of selling.

Direct-Mail is a method of marketing that seems simple on the surface — but can be very complicated. For example, many people think that they understand what Direct-Mail is because they receive many postcards, flyers, and sales letters in the mail. On the surface, it looks so simple and easy but as every marketing expert will tell you — this is a form of marketing that *"takes a day to learn and a lifetime to master."*

In our seminars, I compare Direct-Mail to the game of chess. As you know, there are only six individual chess pieces on the board and each one can only move so many ways... So this game "seems" very simple. And yet there is <u>nothing</u> simple about the game of chess. There are millions of potential moves and many people spend their entire lives mastering this game.

The same is true for Direct-Mail.

On the surface, Direct-Mail seems very simple. For example, most newcomers quickly find out that just one well written sales letter that sells something people really want — can quickly bring in millions of dollars... And this is the gospel truth. In fact, I have personally written Direct-Mail sales letters that have quickly brought in millions of dollars. But what most people do <u>not</u> realize is that...

It usually takes many years of experience to write these powerful Direct-Mail letters that are capable of producing millions of dollars.

It can be very difficult... It's no accident that most of the world's top Direct-Mail copywriters have been in this industry for 10 to 20 years or longer. This makes it very difficult for the newcomer to get rich in Direct-Mail. In fact, all of our first letters that were responsible for the millions we made were either written or re-written by expert Direct-Mail Copywriters like Russ von Hoelscher who had many years of knowledge and experience under their belts.

It took me many years of experience before I was able to write my first Direct-Mail letter that brought us millions of dollars. Developing the right knowledge and skills to be able to bring in millions of dollars from our own Direct-Mail promotions <u>without</u> having any help was the key. The fact that it usually takes many years of experience to be able to write a sales letter that produces millions of dollars is only one problem. There is one problem EVEN BIGGER than this, it's the fact that…

Direct-Mail is very expensive.

Most people think that Direct-Mail is advertising. They're wrong. **A good Direct-Mail letter is all about salesmanship, <u>not</u> advertising.** Why bring this up? Simple. Because the same basic rules that apply to salesmanship are also applicable to Direct-Mail. One of these main principles is:

"The more you tell, the more you sell."

Great salespeople go to great lengths to do a complete job of telling the prospect <u>everything</u> they must know in order to make the sale. Every question and objection the prospect has must be answered. The same is true of a good Direct-Mail offer: If you want the largest number of people to respond to your offer — you <u>must</u> tell the prospect <u>everything</u>. All questions must be answered — or the best prospects will not order.

So here's the biggest problem in a nutshell:

A. If you want to get rich in Direct-Mail — you <u>must</u> tell a

---

complete sales story — from start to finish. Every objection must be overcome. If you don't "tell" enough you won't "sell" enough — and you will lose money.

B. But telling the complete sales story and learning how to write Direct-Mail letters that answer all possible objections can take many years to learn. Many Direct-Mail copywriters had to struggle for years with poor response rates — <u>before</u> they finally developed all of the necessary skills.

But that's not all...

C. Creating a Direct-Mail package that does the most complete job of selling the prospect can be very expensive! Sales letters that are 8 to 12 pages are <u>not</u> uncommon. In fact, sometimes, it takes 24 to 36 page sales letters — with multiple selling devices such as audio CD's and DVD's or multi-sequenced letter writing campaigns to follow up to convert the highest percentage of leads to sales.

All of this can be very costly, time consuming, and requires a great deal of testing and skill...

These problems have made it very difficult to help people get rich in Direct-Mail... _UNTIL_ _NOW_!

For years we have struggled to help our clients make money with Direct-Mail Marketing. This has been very frustrating... On one hand, we <u>knew</u> that Direct-Mail could make many of our Client's large sums of money — just as it has for us. On the other hand — due to the general problems I have just told you about, as well as increase in the prices for postage and good mailing lists, as well as increased competition — **it has been getting <u>harder</u> to make money with Direct-Mail.**

But we were determined to find a way to help our Clients get rich in Direct-Mail... *And now we've done it!*

As you will see. our revolutionary new 'Mailing Co-Op Wealth System' is an amazing new way to get rich in Direct-Mail! This revolutionary new mailing program lets you share a percentage of the total Direct-Mail sales from a group of other mailers who belong to a special 'cooperative group' that we have formed and are managing. Best of all — it's so simple to understand and so easy to use that a 14 year old teenager could make money with this (although all of our Affiliate Partners must be 18 or older to participate).

This new 3-level Affiliate Program makes it possible to do what the title of this book suggests:

To get paid up to $73,150.00, or more, for mailing as few as 1,000 Direct-Mail letters!

Now, mailing 1,000 Direct-Mail letters and getting paid up to $73,150.00 does sound too good to be true — **but please suspend your doubts and disbeliefs for at least 90-minutes and go through this small book very carefully.** You'll see — this very special cooperative Affiliate Mailing Program is built on the best-of-the-best of the same strategies and methods that have brought us over $100 million dollars in DM sales. Now you have the ultimate way to gain the full benefit from all of our years of knowledge and experience. Best of all — we will help you every step of the way.

Although this new 'Mailing Co-Op Wealth System' is simple to understand and easy to do — it does take some time to explain it to you in full so please read carefully.

The next chapter contains the printed transcript of a special Telephone Seminar we recently held for a small group of our best Clients — to tell them all about this exciting new way to make money.

Please read closely. As you'll see, this Tele-Seminar was very exciting!

This was the history making Tele-Seminar that first introduced this amazing new 3-level Affiliate Mailing Program to our Clients — so I wanted you to have it — so you can get the same information they received. Everyone who was on this call that I spoke to later was so excited they couldn't get a good night's sleep for days!

Hopefully, you will be just as excited when you finish reading. So with all that said, let's begin. Please read closely. I have written some special remarks in between the dialog between our Marketing Director, Chris Lakey, and me to make some points more clear and bring out more ideas that we didn't go over... **Plus, you can go to the Web-Site listed at the bottom of each right-hand page of this book to hear the full Tele-Seminar.** So with all this said, let's begin!

ONE LAST WORD... This book was written, typeset, and to the printer in just 10 days. Because of this, it's not perfect. We could've spent ten or even one hundred more days working on it and it <u>still</u> wouldn't be perfect... So please forgive us for any typo's we didn't catch, or writing that's too boring, or not polished enough. **Getting the secrets behind this new Direct-Mail breakthrough into the hands of the people who want to make the maximum amount of money was our #1 priority.** And that leads me to one final money-making idea before ending this Introduction. Here it is: One of the smartest wealth-making experts I know teaches his students that: *"Good enough is good enough."* What does he mean? Simply this: Most of us have a need to make things perfect. We'll work on something forever in an attempt to 'get it just right' <u>when we should be focusing all of our time and energy on doing 'the best job we can, in the fastest period, and then moving on to other things very quickly.'</u> **When it comes to making money, it's the quality of the idea that's important, not the quality of how it is presented.** With this in mind, let's begin.

CHAPTER ONE

The Heavily Edited Printed Transcripts (With Added Commentary) From Our 70-Minute Presentation That Told Our Clients About This Revolutionary New Way To Get Paid up to $73,150.00 For Mailing 1,000 Letters!

NOTE: Printed transcripts of audio recordings can be very difficult to read. Therefore, I went through this carefully and did some rather major editing and re-writing. However, it's important for you to know that my only intention in this major re-writing was to make it easier for you to read these transcripts. Please go to our Web-Site and listen to the unedited recordings, as well as reading this Chapter, to get the full impact of this powerful Direct-Mail business opportunity. Also, please go over my special commentary that you will find at the end of this Chapter. As you'll see, this commentary is rather lengthy, but reading it carefully will help you to better understand the full money-making power of this all new way to potentially make huge sums of money with Direct-Mail Marketing.

So with all this in mind, let's begin…

T.J. ROHLEDER — The title of today's phone call is *"How to*

Make $73,150.00 for Mailing 1,000 Letters." Now I know that sounds too good to be true. But let me just say it one more time: On this call, we're going to give you a brand new Direct-Mail money-making system that allows you to make up to $73,150.00 or more just for mailing 1,000 letters! I don't blame you for being skeptical. But please keep an open mind. If you'll listen very carefully to what we're going to share with you, we will prove that this is the truth in every way. We have based the income projections on conservative estimates, which is something else that we're going to talk about...

Now, first, I do want to give a legal disclaimer:(1) We cannot guarantee and will not guarantee that you will make $73,150.00 or any specific sum of money for mailing a thousand letters or more. However, we have a very solid plan that's based on what we firmly believe are conservative estimates. We're going to show you how everything works. No question will be left unanswered. I just want to make sure that everybody knows that anybody who is being legal and moral and ethical can ever promise you that you will make tens of thousands of dollars or any specific sum of money. That's not what we're doing.

However, this is a plan that (as you'll see) is based on proven strategies. It gives you the best-of-the-best of the methods that have brought tens of millions of dollars to us over the years and, as you'll see, we've put together a complete money-making system that is very revolutionary for you!(2)

So before I get started, let me welcome my co-host — the man who is instrumental in helping me develop this powerful new program. He's the Marketing Director for M.O.R.E., Incorporated. He's also the Marketing Director for the new Direct-Response Network. Mr. Chris Lakey!

Hello Chris.

CHRIS LAKEY — Hey, T. J.! And for you folks listening, this is such a treat because you're going to find out how you can earn up to $73,150.00 or more for every 1,000 letters you mail from home. I know that sounds incredible, but **once you learn how it works I know you'll be as excited as we are and you'll be anxious to learn how to get started.** We're going to tell you all of that. So grab a notepad and a pen and be sure to take lots of notes because we're gonna fly through this fast! There's lots of material to cover. And when we're done you'll know how it all works, <u>and</u> you'll know what to do next to get started… if <u>you</u> are interested in earning up to $73,150.00 or more for every thousand letters you mail from home.

So I'm glad to be here and excited to get started!

T. J. ROHLEDER — Okay! Well thank you, Chris. As always, I couldn't do these calls without you.(3)

Now I want to tell you how we discovered this. A lot of what we put into this new Program has been developed over a period of 19 years. **But the initial spark behind this discovery (that made all of this possible) was made on March the 1st, 2007.** (4) It was the night before our West Coast Pre-Launch Kick-Off Seminar that we held in San Diego, California. I pulled into town on March the 1st and that evening Russ von Hoelscher — the man who made my wife and I millionaires — picked me up at the hotel. We went out for supper at his favorite Mexican Restaurant. Then we went back to my hotel suite and talked until about ten… I think it was 10:30 at night before Russ left, because both of us had to get up early the next morning. By about 10 o'clock that night we were talking about all kinds of ways to make money and, about a half hour before Russ left, he said, *"T. J., I've got something I must tell you about."* He said, *"I've got this* *one promotion that I put together about three years ago and, although I stopped using it after about 10 months...*" (Because he went on to other things.) He said, *"THE MONEY JUST KEEPS COMING IN — WEEK AFTER WEEK AFTER WEEK!"* He said, *"The money just doesn't stop!"*(5) And, of course, I was very interested. I started asking him questions. But it was getting late and he said, *"Hey, I've got one of the Direct-Mail letters at the office."* It's a Direct-Mail package that he said he put together. He said, *"I'll bring it to you tomorrow."* And sure enough, the next day (it was at an all-day and evening seminar on Friday, March 2ⁿᵈ) he gave it to me... I looked at it that night and was so excited by what he had done!

Well, the next day he asked me if I looked at it. I said that I did. Then, that night he took us to a casino in San Diego. While there, I sat at a table across from Russ's office manager, and I started asking her about this Direct-Mail offer and, sure enough, she told me the same thing that Russ said. (Not that I had any doubts that Russ wasn't telling me the truth!) But I just wanted to get her thoughts and feelings about it. She said; *"T. J., the money just keeps coming in every single week!"* These were almost the same words Russ used two nights before. For example, she also said, *"THE MONEY JUST DOESN'T STOP COMING IN!!"*(6)

Well needless to say, I was very excited! I told Russ, *"We've got to talk!"* So the next morning (Sunday morning, March the 3ʳᵈ), Russ came knocking on my door at seven o'clock in the morning and for one hour we sat there and negotiated a deal where he basically let us have this very powerful Direct-Mail promotion he had created and developed. And now we have fine-tuned Russ's discovery, added some of our own ideas and methods to it, and now it's complete and ready to go!!!

Now we're going to do our best to explain what this new

Direct-Mail breakthrough is. But you must know: The basic secret behind this new breakthrough would have never happened if it wasn't for Russ von Hoelscher. **Russ is a genius when it comes to making money.** He's made millions of dollars for my wife, Eileen, and I — especially when we first got started. He has worked with us closely since 1989 and he is absolutely brilliant when it comes to making money. (7)

It all starts with a very special package that we've produced called "THE MILLIONAIRE TRAINING PACKAGE."(8)   This Millionaire Training Package consists of three valuable products and services:

First, we have the 9-hour 'Millionaire Training Audio Program.' This 9-hour program contains our 26 proven secrets that we've used to go from $300.00 back in 1988 to over $100-million dollars in Direct-Mail sales in our first 19 years.

It's a powerful audio program! We spend nine full hours on this audio program giving you the wealth secrets that we have used to bring in many tens of millions of dollars. So all you have to do (if you own this product) is pop those CDs into your car stereo while you're driving around, or play those audio CDs around your house, and it makes it so easy for you to get our 26 greatest wealth-making secrets that truly can make you super rich! And because I normally charge one thousand dollars an hour for my personal consulting (and I have a 3-hour minimum), this program is a bargain at only $495.00.

Chris, before I go on to the other two products, maybe you need to talk about this wonderful 9-hour Millionaire Training Audio Program.

CHRIS LAKEY — Sure, I'd be happy to.

This Program is the foundation of this Millionaire

Training Package because it is like taking a crash course in getting rich in Direct Marketing. There are twenty-six specific wealth-making steps that this powerful audio program takes you through... Because there are 26 letters in the alphabet, we call our 26 secrets: "The A to Z Wealth Formula"(9). You could take each one of those 26 strategies and extrapolate on them and probably spend nine hours on each one! And you could expand on it and make it even bigger than it already is, but this is a bite sized look at 26 top Direct Marketing secrets that have brought us — M.O.R.E., Incorporated — over $100-million dollars in Direct-Response sales.

And so, anybody who wants a crash course in Direct-Response Marketing can get it in this Millionaire Training Audio Program. It's perfect for someone who wants to get started and get a good overview. It's also good for the experienced and seasoned Direct Marketer who's just looking for that extra edge and maybe learning something new. **If you've been in Direct Marketing for any length of time, you know that <u>there's no end to the learning</u>.** And T. J. and I both continue our education. (10) We're getting ready to attend a conference in a month or so, right now, to continue our Direct-Response Marketing education. So either you're brand new and this will help you get off to a good powerful start by learning 26 top secrets or, if you're a seasoned veteran, it will help by just giving you more information. So this is a great starter project... It's the foundation of the Millionaire Training Package. It's a great program, one that you'll be proud to have in any wealth-making collection...

T. J. ROHLEDER — Okay, thank you, Chris.

And, yes, **it is the foundation <u>because</u> it <u>leads</u> <u>to</u> <u>the</u> <u>very</u> next product that's part of our Millionaire Training Package:** This is our two-day workshop called "THE $100-MILLION DOLLAR WORKSHOP."

The purpose of this very special event is to give you the secrets and hands-on help and guidance that you need to make huge sums of money. Many of our past seminars and workshops have sold for as much as $4,985.00. Now think about that. Our Clients have paid almost $5,000.00 to attend our seminars in the past, so the regular value of this workshop is very reasonable. (11) **Coming to a workshop like our $100-MILLION DOLLAR WORKSHOP is the best way that we can share our wealth-making secrets and strategies with you.** Out of all the ways that we have helped people make money over the years, there is no better way than a seminar! This gives us a chance to get to know you better and help you fully.

Chris just told you that we're getting ready to go to a seminar ourselves in less than a month. We paid several thousand dollars to attend that seminar in Chicago. Every year we invest many thousands of dollars to go to other people's seminars to learn.

Chris, there's no better way to teach somebody how to make money than in a seminar format, is there?

CHRIS LAKEY — Well there's something very powerful about being in a room where you're listening to someone present from the front of the room, or several people who are presenting. There's something about being able to talk to people one-on-one and meet and spend time with the people who are teaching you. You know, it's one thing to listen to us on the phone, it's another thing to meet us face-to-face and ask us the questions. We get people at every event who come up to us and ask one question that leads to another question and pretty soon we've spent half an hour with a person, just digging deeper and answering lots of different questions. And sometimes people come and they just get to know us and it helps them know that we're real people and that we're just like them. They see us stand in front of them on stage, we don't wear fancy suits, we're blue jeans people...(12) there's nothing extraordinary about us and that helps them realize that if we can do it, they can do it, too!

And so, there are advantages to coming to a workshop... coming to an event live where you can meet us. And again, that goes for us too. **We continue our education by attending seminars and workshops and, usually, at a cost of many thousands of dollars each time we do it.** And so, there's nothing that can replace coming to these live events... The 9-hour Millionaire Training Audio Program is a good place to start. It is the foundation. Then the workshop takes it to the next level, by allowing you to come and experience our wealth-making teachings firsthand, get to learn more about the ideas we gave you on the training audio program, dig a little bit deeper, and take it to the next level. Again, **that's something that you can't get just listening on audio or reading a book.** You must attend a live workshop to get the kind of hands-on help that can take you from where you are to where you want to go.

MATHEMATICAL INCOME PROJECTION CHART

LEVEL #1 — You mail 1000 MCWS Offers, with just a 1.1% response, 11 new orders come in. You are paid $50.00 each. **Money to you: $550.00.**

Now you are on LEVEL #2 — on this second-level, your 11 new affiliate partners each mail 1000. Total mailings: 11,000, and with the same 1.1% response, 121 orders come in. You get $50.00 x 121. **Money to you: $6,050.00.**

On LEVEL #3 — it becomes exciting! The 121 new affiliate partners each mail 1000 offers. Total mailings: 121,000. A 1.1% response here is 1,331 orders. You get $50.00 x 1,331. **Money to you: $66,550.00.**

You've now completed the 3-level cycle. YOUR TOTAL IS $73,150.00!

T. J. ROHLEDER — Thanks, Chris.

We have had many seminars that have sold for as high as $4,985.00. **So the value we've placed on this two-day "$100-Million Dollar Workshop" is only $3,985.00.** (13) That is based on a conservative value that is comparable to the prices that others are charging for similar events.

Now the third product in our Millionaire Training Package is **a lifetime ground-floor position in our new Multi-Level Marketing opportunity.** This basic level position is valued at $49.95. (14) It is a lifetime position in our new Multi-Level Marketing company, called the Direct-Response Network that's designed to make our Members and our Distributors set for life!

Some of our Distributors and Members are on the phone right now listening to this call so they realize how valuable this is. (15) It is an entry-level position in our Direct-Response Network (not to be confused with the higher level positions in the D.R.N. that offer a greater number of value-added money-making benefits).

Chris, anything to add to that?

CHRIS LAKEY — Well, **this may be the most powerful part of the package.** (16) The more the people who receive our MILLIONAIRE TRAINING PACKAGE know about the Direct-Response Network, the more excited they will be! Of course, people also receive all of the information in the audio program and get the chance to attend the two-day workshop.

And let me throw something out real quick about the workshop... If you can't attend the workshops, we will have the audio available and sometimes you're able to listen in live over the telephone. We <u>always</u> record them on audio CDs so,

---

even if you can't attend live, you're always going to be able to get the audio CDs from any event that we have. **So if you can't make it to Kansas for the $100-MILLION DOLLAR WORKSHOP for whatever reason on the dates of our workshop, you're gonna be able to get them on audio CDs or attend a future event on a date that you can make it. So you don't ever have to worry about missing all of the information we shared with the people who were there.** (17)

But this entry-level position (the third item in our package) gives you a chance to earn commissions with all of the products in our new Multi-Level Marketing company. And we will explain that, of course, more later as we start to reveal to you all of the benefits of this Millionaire Training Package (18). But the important thing to know for now is: **this is something that can pay you a lifetime of ongoing profits.** We'll show you how you can turn that position (without having to pay any more money) into residual income and then in to additional revenues that can come in for months and years to come... just by using that third item: the lifetime ground-floor position in our new MLM opportunity.

T. J. ROHLEDER — Okay!

And so, what we have done is, we have put together a special Distributorship and 3-Level Affiliate Program that lets you offer this Millionaire Training Package to the millions of people who are out there desperately searching for a way to make money! (19) When you add the total value of all three of those products together, you come up with a value of $4,529.95. And that is a conservative price, based on the prices that other people are charging for similar types of products and services. The market is huge. The value of this package is huge. And we have a special sales letter that we have written that does a powerful job of selling this super valuable package. Best of all, this sales letter offers all three of those products for 89% off of the regular price...at the sale price of only $495.00. (20)

And we have a special distributorship called the **'Mailing Co-Op Wealth System'** that is designed to pay you up to $73,150.00 for mailing just 1,000 letters. (21)

Here's how it works: I'm going to go over it very slowly. Then you will get the printed transcripts of today's call so you'll be able to go back and study this and completely understand how all of this works. **There are nine items that I'm going to cover here that shows you how this works,** then I'll pass it to Chris so he can help clear up any confusion that's in the minds of our listeners.

CHRIS LAKEY — Sounds good.

T. J. ROHLEDER — Okay! So here's how you can get paid up to $73,150.00 for mailing just 1,000 letters. (22)

A — You purchase the MILLIONAIRE TRAINING PACKAGE and/or you can sign up as an Affiliate Mailing Partner. When you do this, you'll get the camera-ready sales letter and the order form that sells our $4,529.95 Millionaire Training Package for only $495.00. **$150.00 of that special sale price goes to pay the three Affiliate Mailing Partners who made this offer available to all of the people who are looking for a way to make money.** (23)

B — On the order form are the three names of our Sponsored Affiliates. Your name will be listed in the third position when you get your own camera-ready sales letter and order form from us.

C — You print and mail 1,000 of these letters and order forms or you can let our expert suppliers do it all for you. (24) This means: the total number of mailings with your name in the third position will be 1,000.

D — You receive a 1.1% response (just as an example) for the 1,000 letters that you mail and that comes to 11 Direct-Mail sales total. **And you're paid a commission of $50.00 on every package sold, which comes out to $550.00 total.**

E — Those 11 people also receive a camera-ready sales letter and an order form with your name in the second position in the Sponsored Affiliate box. So now all they do is mail 1,000 letters — or they let our experts do it all for them — and the total number of mailings now, with your name in the second position is, 11,000.

F — As an example, let's say that they also receive a 1.1% response on those 11,000 letters that they mailed. That would come to 121 people who order the product, which is the MILLIONAIRE TRAINING PACKAGE, and also become Affiliates. **You are paid a commission of $50.00 for each package sold, and that comes out to $6,050.00 total.**

G — These 121 people <u>also</u> receive a camera-ready sales letter and order form with your name moved all the way to the first position in the Sponsored Affiliate box. Now they mail a thousand letters — **or they let our experts mail those letters for them.** And the total number of mailings that you have now, with your name in the very first position, is 121,000 letters! Think about that.

H — As an example, if they also received a 1.1% response, that's a total of 1,331 new people who order the same Millionaire Training Package and become Affiliate Mailing Partners, **and you're paid a commission of $50.00 for each package sold:** <u>**That comes to $66,550.00 in your pocket**</u>**!**

I — When you combine the total income for all three Affiliate Positions, it comes out to $73,150.00! (24)

Now I have to disclaim this again: All of these Mathematical Income Projections are based on a 1.1% response rate. We cannot guarantee that everybody will get 1.1% response. (25) And, we cannot guarantee that everyone is going to mail a thousand letters. However, if everybody mails a thousand letters — and if everybody just gets an average of 1.1% response to all of those letters that they mail, we can say with complete confidence that it is potentially possible to earn as much as $73,150.00 for mailing just 1,000 letters. PLUS, because we've got such a powerful offer that really does give people a value of $4,529.95 for 89% off the regular price, **we're doing everything within our power to give you and your Affiliate Partners a percentage of 1.1% response. Getting this kind of percentage of response is not uncommon at all when you've got a great offer and you mail it to the right mailing lists.** We have mailed millions of pieces of Direct-Mail over the years and when you've got a hot offer (something that people really want), it's not uncommon at all to get a response rate of 1.1 percent. All you do is mail a thousand pieces of mail.

If you get a 1.1% response — and we supply everything for you (26) — then you'll have 11 sales of the MILLIONAIRE TRAINING PACKAGE from people who also want to become Affiliate Mailing Partners. Those 11 people can duplicate the process by mailing one thousand Direct-Mail packages. Now you've got 11,000 pieces of mail out there — plus the original thousand you mailed. And if all 11 of your Affiliate Mailing Partners gets an average of 1.1% response rate again, then now you will have 121 Affiliates, (27) plus the original 11 that you already attracted as a result of your own 1,000 piece mailing. Now those 121 people can duplicate the process. **If they also receive an average of 1.1% response, you will now be in the powerful position to get paid on a**

---

total of 133,000 pieces of mail with your name on the order form as the Affiliate Sponsor who is scheduled to be paid!

With a 1.1% response on all three levels (assuming that everyone mails 1,000 pieces and you get an average of 1.1% response) and you're getting paid $50.00 on <u>every</u> single order, that comes out to $73,150.00.

Chris, I can't think of anything more exciting than the way this whole thing works together... <u>the leverage that it creates</u> (28) <u>where everybody mails a thousand pieces</u>. And if everybody just gets a minimum of just 1.1%, which means that 989 people out of every 1,000 throw the envelopes away. (29) They don't even read it. They trash it! And everybody just gets 11 people out of 1,000 to go ahead and respond and to take the offer. There is an opportunity for people to make $73,150.00 for only mailing 1,000 pieces of Direct-Mail!

In all your years, Chris, and I know you've been around this business for over half of your life, isn't that about the most exciting thing you've ever heard?

CHRIS LAKEY — Most definitely!

This is something that, you know, I wish we had thought of... I wish Russ would have brought to us a long time ago. You know? It just shows you the power of, again, being together in a room with people. **Had we not went to San Diego and been sitting there face-to-face with Russ, maybe he wouldn't have taken the time to share this story and maybe we're not sitting here today being able to present this.** (30)

But certainly it's a powerful plan. And the thing that I like about it is that <u>it's</u> <u>so</u> <u>simple</u> <u>to</u> <u>understand</u>...<u>and</u> <u>yet</u> <u>so</u> <u>powerful</u>! If you think about it like an affiliate program on the Internet — which is really all it is — it's a three-tiered affiliate program. And just like on the Internet where you sign someone up as an affiliate, they help sell your product, and then that person also has someone they know who might be interested in selling the product. And so then you have a two-tiered affiliate program where that person can go out and make a sale and two people get paid an affiliate commission for making that sale. This is a three-tiered affiliate program. (31) **It's just an affiliate program that, instead of being on the Internet, is done by Direct-Mail...which we feel is more powerful and gives it a greater chance for long-term success because we know how to make Direct-Mail work.** (32)

And so what you've got here is an ability, with a three-tier affiliate program, to just mail a small number of Direct-Mail letters...have people sign up as an affiliate...buy the product... and, again, just using mathematical projections of 1.1% response shows you how this has the potential to make you a lot of money... You know, we sometimes get as high as a 5% response for our own Direct-Mail. Sometimes we get as low as half a percent response. The response rate is just meant to be an average. But 1.1% is certainly a pretty conservative estimate. Of course, when you mail a thousand letters you may get less than 1.1% or you may get more than 1.1%. But that's just an average. You know, 1.1%...you get just 11 people to respond out of your initial 1,000 letters that you mail. And those 11 people, when the system works out like this mathematical example, can potentially turn into a total of $73,150.00.... It's just a tremendous opportunity!

Most people can mail a thousand letters. (33) So, think about how easy it is to just drop a thousand letters in the mail on your own or we've got suppliers who are ready, willing, and able to do that for you, too. We'll be talking about that in a little bit. So when you think about how easy it is to mail a thousand letters and let other people basically duplicate the same steps, you'll see how amazingly powerful this is. These

MATHEMATICAL INCOME PROJECTION CHART

LEVEL #1 — You mail 1000 MCWS Offers, with just a 1.1% response, 11 new orders come in. You are paid $50.00 each. **Money to you: $550.00.**

Now you are on **LEVEL #2** — on this second-level, your 11 new affiliate partners each mail 1000. Total mailings: 11,000, and with the same 1.1% response, 121 orders come in. You get $50.00 x 121. **Money to you: $6,050.00.**

On **LEVEL #3** — it becomes exciting! The 121 new affiliate partners each mail 1000 offers. Total mailings: 121,000. A 1.1% response here is 1,331 orders. You get $50.00 x 1,331. **Money to you: $66,550.00.**

You've now completed the 3-level cycle. YOUR TOTAL IS $73,150.00!

people can become your Affiliates and, as we've explained, just three affiliate levels and a total of 121,000 pieces of mail going out with your third affiliate level...and <u>you have just turned 1,000 letters into 121,000 letters</u>. And if everyone gets an average of a 1.1% response (as an example only); on your third affiliate level your Affiliate Mailing Partners would sell 1,331 packages which would earn you $66,550.00. Your total would come out to a whopping $73,150.00!

It seems like the only real question people want to know is how they can get their thousand letters and mail them out!

T. J. ROHLEDER — Well yes! Yes! And now let's talk about the benefits of the program. Then as we wrap up this call today, we'll go over the mathematical income projections one more time and help everybody understand this.

The first benefit is: This is 100% legal, moral, and ethical... (34)

Like Chris said, the Internet is filled with one-tier and two-tier affiliate programs. They're everywhere. All you have to do is go on any search engine, type in the words; "affiliate programs," and you'll see, there are many of these programs that are two-tiered. What we've done is added a third tier and used Direct-Mail instead of the Internet to sell our MILLIONAIRE TRAINING PACKAGE. **It is so exciting, but I want you to know this is totally legal, it's moral, it's ethical, and it's a real business. It's not some kind of gambling or lottery scheme.** Again, it's a three-level affiliate program. To keep it legal, we allow people to become affiliates without the mandatory purchase of the MILLIONAIRE TRAINING PACKAGE. So I want everybody to feel assured that you're getting involved in something that is 100% legal. Letting people become Affiliates Mailing Partners without purchasing the Millionaire Training Package is the key distinction that makes this regulatory friendly. And the fact is that the product that is the foundation of this Program really is worth $4,529.95 — but you're offering it for 89% off of the regular price! That is one of the best things we have built into this Affiliate Mailing Program to get everybody sky-high percentage rates!

Again, all you need is 1.1% response on the thousand letters that you mail and all of your Affiliate Partners mail. If everybody is mailing a thousand letters and if everybody is just getting 1.1% response on average, you now have the potential to earn as much as $73,150.00 for mailing 1,000 letters... Like Chris said, some lists pull 3% and some lists pull half of 1%. Some lists pull maybe 5%. Some lists don't even produce any percent because there are some dud lists out there. But as long as your overall response rate averages out to a little over one percent, then the overall sum of money that can be earned is enormous... **And if you're working with our suppliers, we mix up all of these lists. We shuffle it like a deck of cards so we're mixing the lists up so we make sure**

that nobody gets a dud list. (35)   But if everybody just averages 1.1%, which is only 11 sales for every thousand pieces of mail, then the numbers simply don't lie.   If everybody is just doing their small part, you've got the ability here to mail 1,000 pieces of Direct-Mail... and because you're getting paid not only on those thousand pieces that you mail, but assuming you get 1.1% response, you're also getting paid a generous commission on the 1,000 pieces that those 11 Affiliates of yours mail and the 121 people on your second tier.   You're getting paid for all of that, too.   So, it's tremendous and it is legal.

Chris, anything to add to that?

CHRIS LAKEY — There's a lot of trash out there.   There's a lot of people who come up with an idea for some way to make money and they throw something together real quick.   So you do have to be careful.   So we're not trying to scare you by telling you that there are things out there that aren't legal, we're just trying to show you that what we're doing is 100% legal, moral, and ethical... This is simply an affiliate program that pays on three tiers and, instead of being online like a lot of two-tier affiliate programs are, we're using Direct-Mail to make the sale.   So it's probably one of only a very small number of offline affiliate programs.

I am actually an affiliate of another program... a Web-Site that has a bunch of information products that I think are high quality and they actually allow you to sell by mail and by phone or on the Internet, the traditional way.   And so there are other products that you can sell by mail that you can be an affiliate for.   But there are not very many affiliate programs that are similar to ours... So people just have to stop and think, *"Okay, I know what an affiliate program is on the Internet.* ***This is just an affiliate program that's not on the Internet."*** So it pays you on three levels... three affiliate levels.   And it pays the same on all three levels, so it's $50.00 for each of the three positions. That means we pay $150.00 on every $495.00 sale and that $150.00 goes to the three affiliates who are in affiliate position one, affiliate position two, and affiliate position three — just like we talked about. And having the ability to be an affiliate without buying the products is important for legal reasons. There are some good reasons to do that, too. You know, if people just want to sell the products, we must give them the opportunity just to sell the products without enjoying and using the products. But **I don't know why anybody would want to be an affiliate and sell the products without knowing what the products were and being able to have said that they use them themselves as well.** (36) So hopefully a lot of people will want to buy and use the products, as well as be an Affiliate. Again, all it takes is a 1.1% response, in this example, for that to add up on a thousand letters mailed by all of the Affiliates, to total $73,150.00.

T. J. ROHLEDER — Yeah, that is so exciting!

I'm going fast here, Chris, because I'm watching the clock.

The second benefit is: You have the opportunity to get paid huge sums of money from very small numbers of response.

You get paid huge profits for mailing just a small number of letters and for only getting a small percentage of response. So remember, our $73,150.00 example is based on only a 1.1% response. That's only 11 sales for every 1,000 letters that you and your Affiliate Partners mail. And that means if as many as 989 people out of every 1,000 throw your letters and your affiliate partners' letters in the trashcan — assuming that everybody mails a thousand letters — you're still going to be in the position to make $73,150.00!

Think about this: You mail a thousand letters and 989 of those people throw it away. These 987 people don't even bother looking at it. **However, if only 11 of those people will go ahead and take the Millionaire Training Package from you and from all of your affiliates — assuming that you all mail just a thousand pieces — you're still going to get paid $73,150.00!** (37)

Chris, this ought to keep people up at night if they really think about it, won't it?

CHRIS LAKEY — Absolutely!

But don't think about the 133,000 letters that could be mailed on all three affiliate levels. Just think about the 1,000 that you're responsible for and that you can be in control of and let everything else take care of itself. (38) But just 1,000 letters that you mail out can turn into $73,150.00 — according to this example (at a 1.1% response, with everybody else doing their part and also mailing a thousand letters). **The numbers add up so quickly and it makes for a powerful marketing vehicle to help us sell our products and pay you huge commissions for doing your part as an Affiliate.** The numbers add up and it just gets so huge so fast. And yet, it's all based on you just mailing a thousand letters and getting a very modest 1.1% response.

Of course, you can play with the numbers if you want to grab a calculator and think about it in your own mind or jot it down on some paper... (39) What would happen if it wasn't 1.1? What if it was 2%? Or what if it was 3%? Or what if it was only .8%? You know? Play around with the numbers a little bit. It gets real exciting and it can drive you nuts at the same time because you start thinking: *"Wow, I wonder whether I will get 1% or whether I will get 1.1. or whether I'll get 2 or 3% like we have gotten on some things in the past or whether I'll only get .8 or .7?"* Play with the numbers and see what happens. You'll be so excited! We've used 1.1% because it's a good middle-of-the-road average. Of course, like T. J. said, we can't guarantee that you would get 1.1% or even any percentage specifically because each mailing list is different and some lists get 1.1% and some get 2% or 3%. We've had lists get as high as 5% and some lists get as low as... Well, we've had lists totally bomb in the past, to be honest with you, sometimes a list just stinks. (40)

Like T. J. said, our mailing house can do the same thing for you that they do for us. **They 'feather the mailing lists' so if we have a bunch of different lists we're testing, it limits our risks...** For example, let's say if we were mailing a thousand letters like this example, they actually work it so that they might be mailing 100 pieces...a hundred names...a hundred addresses from 10 different lists to get the thousand. (41). **Instead of mailing a thousand names and address from one list, they would mail a hundred from ten different lists to get the thousand (just as an example).** But play with the numbers. It gets real exciting to think about the potential when you just mail a thousand letters and then let everything else work its magic like the system is set up to do.

T. J. ROHLEDER — Yeah, it is so exciting! The more you'll do what Chris just said, grab a calculator and play with this yourself, you'll see that this has got to be the most exciting home-based business opportunity in the world!

I'm going cover the next two benefits in one stab and then pass it to you, Chris.

Benefit number three: This is proven.

As I said in the beginning of today's call: Our company has brought in over $100-million dollars in Direct-Mail sales. Direct-Mail is our primary marketing vehicle. We have done a little space advertising and some stuff on the Internet, but Direct-Mail is our preferred marketing method. This is what we specialized in. **And the sales letter that you will be mailing, to offer our Millionaire Training Package for 89% off the regular price, is based on the same basic kind of sales letter that we've used to make our own fortune.** Chris and I are responsible for bringing in tens of millions of dollars worth of Direct-Mail sales and we are the ones who wrote the sales letter that you'll be using. So you're gaining from our multi-million dollar experience! (42)

Benefit number four: You're getting total leverage wealth-making power.

What do I mean by that? Simply this: All you and your Affiliate Partners do is mail a thousand letters. Again, you're averaging a little over 1% response. And if that happens, you're gonna be eligible to receive a commission that's based on a grand total of 133,000 letters that are mailed. And that's with just each person just mailing a thousand.

Now, **most people could never afford to mail 133,000 pieces of Direct-Mail.** (43) But because you and your Affiliate Partners are working together (through us managing the whole thing for you) it now becomes possible for all of you do to this. Unfortunately, Direct-Mail is very expensive. For years we've wanted to help people get rich in Direct-Mail, but the cost is prohibitive for most people. But finally, with this powerful 'Mailing Co-Op Wealth System' that we've developed, it's possible for all of you to share in the combined resources of all of you mailing together. (44) So you're not only getting paid on all of the 1,000 Direct-Mail letters that you mail, but it also lets you get paid on all of the letters they mail. **We're more than happy to pay you and all of your Affiliate Partners a commission of $150.00 total on every sale because you'll be helping us reach customers for our Millionaire Training Package that we would not be able to reach without your help.** (45) So it's a win/win/win situation! You win because you've got an opportunity — you and your affiliate partners have an opportunity to each mail just a thousand Direct-Mail letters. And as we've shown you, the potential is here to make up to $73,150.00 or more, for only mailing a relatively small number of letters! Your customers win because the people who are getting the Millionaire Training Package will get the ultimate wealth training available for a super low price! This is an exciting package that's worth $4,529.95. Everybody gets it for 89% off. And just coming to Kansas to attend our two-day workshop, that alone, can change people's lives! (46) We can help people in a powerful kind of way. And then our company wins because we put all of this together. **Both you and your Affiliate Mailers are helping us to reach a broader market. You're helping us to get our Millionaire Training Package into the hands of many people, and we're more than happy to reward you and your Affiliate Partners in the greatest way.** (47)

Chris?

CHRIS LAKEY — You explained it well. We've got a system here that lets you make money by mailing a thousand letters. And, again, the math all works out (based on this average of 1.1% response) to $73,150.00. The math will change as the numbers change. The numbers that you really achieve will be different than the example that we've shared with you here.(48) But it all starts with mailing a thousand letters. And again, it gives you a chance to allow our Affiliates — you — to do the work and mail a thousand letters and make these sales for us. **We're happy to reward you with this compensation plan because you are doing the work to get those thousand letters into the marketplace to make the whole system work like we've set it up to so that you get paid and the other Affiliates get paid just by mailing as few as one thousand letters.** Or, if you want to mail more than that, you're welcome to mail more than a thousand letters. But it's set up to pay you by working the system and the system is based on mailing one thousand letters. And if you'll do that, then we're happy to pay you and happy to reward you for the results that you achieve with the system.

MATHEMATICAL INCOME PROJECTION CHART

LEVEL #1 — You mail 1000 MCWS Offers, with just a 1.1% response, 11 new orders come in. You are paid $50.00 each. **Money to you: $550.00.**

Now you are on LEVEL #2 — on this second-level, your 11 new affiliate partners each mail 1000. Total mailings: 11,000, and with the same 1.1% response, 121 orders come in. You get $50.00 x 121. **Money to you: $6,050.00.**

On LEVEL #3 — it becomes exciting! The 121 new affiliate partners each mail 1000 offers. Total mailings: 121,000. A 1.1% response here is 1,331 orders. You get $50.00 x 1,331. **Money to you: $66,550.00.**

You've now completed the 3-level cycle. YOUR TOTAL IS $73,150.00!

T. J. ROHLEDER — Okay. And, Chris, I'm going to cover Benefit Five and then hand it to you for Benefit Six.

Benefit five is: This is just so simple and easy to do.

I know I'm sounding like a broken record, but all you have to do is just mail a thousand of the letters. You get the 8-page letter and order forms from us and, within just a couple of weeks of time, just working a little bit every day, you can put a thousand pieces of mail in the mail within no time at all. These envelopes mail for under an ounce so you're only using one First Class postage stamp. (49) **It's so simple, it's so easy — unlike most business that are very complicated.**

And yet, **Benefit Number Six makes it even easier. Chris, why don't you explain that one?**

Like T. J. said, you're welcome to take our 8-page sales letter and the order form then mail a little bit every day or a little bit every week and, depending on how much energy and effort you put into it, you might be able to get a thousand letters in the mail in a week or it might take you a month or more. You know, when you just do a little bit here and there it adds up and you can do that. **Or, you can let our suppliers do everything for you — and they're ready, willing, and able.** They're more than capable of doing that because they do it for us every day. (50) We work with a mailing house and a printer on a daily basis. They attend our weekly meetings where we schedule the mailings that go out on a regular basis. Our printer makes the almost hour drive one-way to our office every single day, Monday through Friday. He knows our business and what we do almost as well as we do! And so, both of them work hand-in-hand; our mailing house and our printer. And in this case, if you would like them to, they'll do that for you. They will do everything for you. **Our mailing house will rent the mailing lists that they need to mail this offer out for you. They will work with our printer to have the sales letter printed on the right kind of paper to get the best postage rates, to get the right weight of paper.** <u>We print the sales letter on newsprint</u>. It's a much lighter paper and that makes it easier to print it for the lowest cost and mail for the lowest cost (51) because it gets the weight down over regular copy paper that you would get if you printed these letters at a Kinko's or Office Max.

So our printer does all of that. They deliver the sales letters and your own custom-printed order forms to our mailing house and our mailing house takes it from there. They insert your sales letters and order forms into the envelope. They do all of the printing on the envelope, not with labels that look cheap, you know, but instead, it looks like a package you get in the mail that was done on a home computer. The names are actually laser printed right on the envelope. **Everything is done professionally. They deliver your sales letters, your custom-printed order forms to the mailing house... Then the whole package gets delivered to the Post Office. They sort it right so you get the best postage rates. Rather than just sticking a regular First Class stamp on it and paying the highest rate possible, they sort it to get the best rate possible — which saves you money on postage, as well.** They do all that for you. (52)

You can let these expert suppliers do it all, so that you don't have to worry about it. All you do is check the box on the form we give you. They'll take it from there and do it all for you. They'll go to work for you, just like they do for us. They rent the mailing lists for us, get us the best postage rates, and take care of it all. **Our printer and our mailing house work together to make sure it happens on time, and all for the lowest price possible.** And that same service that they've been delivering for us for many, many, many years…they can deliver for you through this service, so that you don't have to do any of the work yourself. **They can do everything while you sit back and wait for the results to come in.** (53)

We will pay you a commission of $50.00 — each and every time an order form comes in with your name on it… Yes, you will earn a $50.00 commission through this compensation plan that pays you on three affiliate levels — depending on whether you're in position number one, two, or number three. (54) It works like clockwork. And you can choose to do it all yourself; we'll give you all the sales letters and everything you need. Or, you can let our suppliers do it all for you while you sit back and wait for it all to work. So that's that.

T. J. ROHLEDER — Well thank you, Chris.

And we have a special **Affiliate Start-Up Package** that

contains all of the materials that makes it so simple and easy for you to get started. (55) Again, you're using the same suppliers that we have used to mail millions of Direct-Mail pieces. These people are capable, they're competent, they're honest. You can depend on them. They will work for you, just like they work for us on a regular basis. Or you can mail them all yourself. The choice is yours.

Benefit number seven: The start-up cost is super low.

What other business can you start for the cost of mailing a thousand Direct-Mail letters that has the potential to make you as much money as this one does? (56) Study the numbers. And in the book that we'll create that's based on today's audio program, we're going to print the Mathematical Income Projection Chart that proves to you that all it takes is just mailing a thousand pieces of mail and getting a response of a little over 1 percent, and then for your Affiliates to each do the very same thing. And now you're in a position to make $73,150.00. It's so exciting!! **The cost is low and the potential profits are very high!**

Chris, anything to add about the low cost?

CHRIS LAKEY — Well, yeah, most businesses struggle to ever make any real money. And there are business owners who probably would have been better off staying in their regular day jobs. They sweat it out, working long hours, working weekends, putting in a ton of work to never make anywhere near $73,150.00 in a year, let alone the kind of money that's possible to be made with this system... (57) Again, it's just in the mathematical example... but **how long would it take you to mail a thousand letters? And how long would it take the other people who are your Affiliate Mailing Partners to mail a thousand letters for you?** (58) Once that happens (however long or short of an amount of time that takes), you've got the potential to make $73,150.00 if it all worked out like this mathematical example. So this really is an extremely low start-up cost when you stop to consider the potential you have to make (in this example, again) up to $73,150.00 just by mailing a thousand letters.

T. J. ROHLEDER — Well absolutely.

And last, but not least, **the eighth benefit is: We do everything possible to help you and all of your Affiliate Mailing Partners make the very most money.**

Our success is tied to your success. All business opportunity promoters 'claim' they want to help you make money. But when you ask them, *"What's in it for you?"* many of those people give you answers that are unclear. (59) Well we're telling you <u>exactly</u> what's in it for us! Through the combined efforts of you and all of your Affiliate Mailing Partners, we are going to reach a much wider audience for our Millionaire Training Package (60) (that, when you combine those three products that make up this package, it has a value of <u>$4,529.95</u>). You guys are selling it for 89% off the regular price, so you're giving people a tremendous deal. You're using sales material that was developed by two copywriters who have a history of bringing in tens of millions of dollars in Direct-Mail sales. (61) Plus, as you can see, we've put together a tremendous offer, in an attempt to do everything we can to help you and your Affiliate Mailing Partners get an average of 1.1% response.

And now, we're going to go further than that!

You see, we're also going to provide on-going training and on-going support and help for all of the people that are your Affiliate Partners, to help them make the most amount of money! We will be giving your Affiliate Mailing Partners (who also take the MILLIONAIRE TRAINING PACKAGE) the best-of-the-best of the tips, tricks, and strategies that have made us millions of dollars. This is the ultimate way to help them and you! (62) Getting this hands-on training is one of the reasons why we encourage all of our Affiliates to purchase and use our Millionaire Training Package.

We want you and your Affiliate Mailing Partners to come to Kansas. We want to get to know you. We want to work with you. We want to help you! **Our best secrets for making millions of dollars can be your best secrets for making millions of dollars.** Plus, we want people to be very proud of the product that they're selling by mail. (63)

However, we are letting people become Affiliate Mailing Partners without purchasing the product, so it's not mandatory that they do make this purchase. (64) But for those who do buy the package, we're going to go out of our way to give them the personal hands on help, support, and guidance they need to make the largest sum of money. We want to help people in the fullest way, and that will involve them (hopefully) coming to Kansas, participating in the $100-Million Dollar Workshop, getting to know us a little bit, letting us work with them. And here's the ultimate thing; **Through the process of training you and all of your Affiliate Mailing Partners, we will do our best to encourage all of you to take a percentage of the money you make with our Mailing Co-Op Wealth System and to put it back into more Direct-Mailings.** (65) You don't have to do this. The choice is yours. We have shown you that it's potentially possible to just mail a thousand pieces of mail, to get a response rate of a little over 1%, and then to have all of your Affiliate Partners do the very same thing, and a chance here for you to make incredible amounts of money! But we're going to do everything possible to work with you and your Affiliate Mailing Partners, to get them to mail that same thousand pieces of mail on a regular basis... We'll encourage them to take a percentage of every dollar that they bring in and put it into a thousand more mailings...and a thousand more. **So the amount of money that you could potentially make from your Affiliate Partners... (through the ongoing help, support, and guidance and encouragement they get from us) those people could not just mail a thousand pieces, or they could mail a thousand pieces every 90 days, or a thousand pieces every 6 months, or a thousand pieces a month!** We can't promise or guarantee it, but once your Affiliate Mailing Partners realize the tremendous value of 'pyramiding their profits' and putting a percentage of their money back into more mailings, they could ultimately mail a thousand pieces a week! But no matter how many Direct-Mail packages they do mail, one thing is certain: your name will always be on each one of the Order Forms that they mail, so that you will get paid a $50.00 commission, each and every time somebody purchases our Millionaire Training Package for 89% off the regular price. The money you can make can keep getting paid to you forever! (66) And you can count on us, to always be here to do everything we can to help you and your Affiliate Partners make the largest sum of money possible.

Chris, what can you add to that?

CHRIS LAKEY — Well, to some degree, you can tell what a company or a person is going to do in the future, based on what they have done in the past. So when we say, *"We will do everything possible to help you and the other Affiliates make the most money"*, you can count on it because that's what we <u>always</u> do! (67) We've always provided above and beyond the support necessary for all of the systems and opportunities that we've been researching and reporting to our Clients since 1988. And you can rest assured that in the future, with this opportunity, we will continue doing the same thing and providing great service. And what that means is that as we continue to develop this. We will be here to help you if you have questions or just need some feedback... If you ever wonder about something or have a quick question or whatever, we're here for you. PLUS, we're also here to continue researching and finding ways to improve this powerful opportunity and make it even better. (68)

Again, helping people make money is something that we've prided ourselves on since the day that we first began researching and publishing business opportunities back in 1988. And you can count on us for continued great service and great support!

T. J. ROHLEDER — Well, Chris, I want to thank you for helping to make all of this clear. I want to give you some parting comments here in just a moment, but I could never do these weekly calls without you, Chris. So thank you very much.

CHRIS LAKEY — Absolutely.

T. J. ROHLEDER — Okay.

And now, I just want to take one more chance to explain this program and clear up any confusion you may have... I know we've covered a lot of ground here. But for those of you that were skeptical an hour ago when we told you that this was a potential for you to get paid up to $73,150.00 or more for just mailing 1,000 Direct-Mail letters, now you know that this is real and solid. **But maybe you're still are a little skeptical, so let me just quickly again go over just some of the basics:** (69)

We have a special product called "The Millionaire Training Package." It consists of three products: First is our Millionaire Training Audio Program, valued at $495.00. The second is our two day '$100-Million Dollar Workshop,' valued at $3,985.00. And the third is an Entry-Level Lifetime Position in our new Multi-Level Marketing company, that sells for $49.95. When you take the three of those together, it's a true value of $4,529.95.

Then we have written a powerful sales letter that lets you sell this package for 89% off the regular price. So the special sale price is only $495.00. And on top of that, (and this is the key to making up to $73,150.00 or more for mailing a thousand letters) we have a three level Affiliate Program called **"The Mailing Co-Op Wealth System"** that lets you mail a thousand of the Direct-Mail letters that sells this product. So if you just would average, as an example, 1.1% response (of people who buy the product and also choose to become Affiliate Mailing Partners), you'd have 11 buyers — and you get $50.00 commission, which is $550.00. Nothing to write home about, but now you're on level two. And on the second level your 11 new Affiliate Partners each mail a thousand of their own Direct-Mail letters. Now your total mailings are 11,000 and with the same 1.1% response, that's 121 orders that come in. You get $50.00 times 121, so the money paid to you on that level is $6,050.00. Now it's getting a little more exciting. But on level three is where it really heats up, because now you have 121 new Affiliate Partners who each mail a thousand of the letters. That's total mailings of 121,000. And a 1.1% response rate here is 1,331 orders. Again, you're getting $50.00 each on all 1,331 of those orders. So that's money paid to you of $66,650.00. You've now completed your three level cycle and your total income is $73,150.00!

So, Chris, we've run out of time. I don't blame anybody for being skeptical about this when we started this call an hour ago. But now they can see that it's more than possible from purely a mathematical example to get paid $73,150.00 for mailing 1,000 letters. **And because we do everything possible to combine the best-of-the-best of everything that we've developed since 1988 to generate over $100-million dollars in Direct-Mail sales, and we've combined it together to this powerful offer that's designed to give people that 1.1% response**, it is more than possible to make

huge sums of money for doing a small number of mailings —
although we cannot guarantee and cannot promise that our
participants will make $73,150.00 or any specific sum, it is
possible to make huge sums of money.

Anything to add to that, Chris?

CHRIS LAKEY — I just want to encourage people to do their own
math. Start with a thousand letters and figure a 1.1%
response. Play around with it. What happens if it's 1.5?
What if it's 2 or 3 percent? Or what if it's 5 percent? <u>What
if it's only half a percent? Play around with the numbers a
little bit on each level.</u> **Remember, there are three affiliate
levels... so you can quickly and easily do the math.** And
consider that everybody is going to mail out a thousand letters
(as an example), play around with the different percentages,
look at how exciting this can be, and then follow our
instructions to make sure that you mail <u>your</u> thousand letters
and start the whole process. It's this simple and easy!

T. J. ROHLEDER — Yes! And we've got an Affiliate Start-Up
Package that makes everything crystal clear. It explains
everything. And the recordings we're doing today are going
be part of a book called "*How To Get Paid $73,150.00 For
Mailing 1,000 Letters!*"

So, we thank Russ von Hoelscher for introducing this amazing
Direct-Mail breakthrough to us. As you have (hopefully)
seen, this is a revolutionary new opportunity that has the
potential power to make you huge sums of money! I am
convinced that many of the people that are listening to this
are going to make hundreds of thousands of dollars with this
program, although I cannot and will not promise that they will
make this amount, or any specific money. I know in my heart
this is gonna make some people very rich. So thank you guys
for listening.

Here Is My Detailed Commentary, Based On All The Ideas We Shared During Our Special Presentation

These ideas will help you further understand the presentation that was given by Chris Lakey and myself. Please find the corresponding numbers in the printed transcripts of our presentation. With that in mind, please read closely...

(1) Please go over the 'IMPORTANT LEGAL NOTICE' in the beginning of this book. You'll see; all of the specific income figures in this book are based on mathematical projections and are NOT a guarantee or promise that you will make these specific amounts of money. It's so important that you realize this. Nobody can ever guarantee or promise that you will make any specific sum of money in this or any other business opportunity, and this is NOT what we are doing. You must understand and accept this fully. As in every business opportunity; there are certain risks involved. Your own income will always vary. However, on a personal note, I must also say that out of the thousands of business plans I have researched and tested, this one is the most exciting! Please read carefully and see if you don't agree. Also, as the title of this Chapter says: I have taken the liberty to heavily edit the text, to make it more readable. You can go to our Web-Site and listen to the actual recording and read along as you listen... However, you must know that **the only reason I have greatly edited the text of our presentation was to make this more readable for all the people who will NEVER listen to the actual recording.**

(2) We have taken the best-of-the-best of all the methods that we

have used to make tens of millions of dollars in Direct-Mail sales and put them into this amazingly simple, but extremely powerful new money-making plan. Although this is no promise that you will make millions of dollars or any specific sum of money or even any money, **it is a major benefit you should carefully consider, that separates this business plan from all the others** (which were developed by people with no knowledge, no experience, and no proven track record of past performance).

(3)   **Chris Lakey is the Marketing Director of our company; 'Mid-American Opportunity Research Enterprises, Inc. (M.O.R.E. Incorporated, for short) and for our new company; The Direct-Response Network.** He started in our shipping department when he was only 16 years old and worked his way up to the top of the company, right under me. Somewhere along the way, Chris fell in love with our business. Once that happened, he became a great marketer! Now he is only 32 years old and yet he has been in and around our Direct-Response Marketing business for over HALF of his life! He is a vital part of our operation, and has played a major role in the development of this revolutionary new way to get rich in the Direct-Mail industry.

(4)   We will continue to test and fine-tune this money-making system for all our Affiliate Mailing Partners. We will do regular testing, in an attempt to make it EVEN MORE POWERFUL. **All our Partners will benefit greatly from these on-going tests and experimentations we make and share in all of the future breakthrough developments.**

(5)`It was MUSIC TO MY EARS when Russ von Hoelscher told me *"The money just keeps coming in — week after week after week!"* And *"The money just doesn't stop!"* I got very excited! Even though I had a 3-day Seminar to participate in that started the next day, THIS WAS ALL I COULD THINK ABOUT!!! I had to know more! And now I'm even more excited! Yes, I get more excited about this amazing new way to get rich in Direct-Mail every single day! The more you know about this, the more excited you'll be, too!

(6) Our company has been researching business and money-making opportunities since 1988 and reporting our research to many thousands of Clients. Over the years, **THE BIGGEST WEALTH-MAKING BREAKTHROUGHS we have ever discovered (the ones that produced many millions of dollars in a short period of time) were made by 'keeping my ear to the ground' and talking closely with the movers and shakers like Russ von Hoelscher.** Russ is a MASTER at turning small sums of money into a huge fortune; so when he talks, we listen! His tips, tricks, and strategies have made us huge sums of money over the years... But this new discovery for getting paid up to $73,150.00 for mailing as few as 1,000 Direct-Mail letters is his ultimate money-making breakthrough!

(7) When it comes to making money, you should only listen to and take advice from people who have a proven track record for making a lot of money. **These are the only people who can really help you.** Now, having said this; there is nobody smarter and more talented when it comes to developing specific strategies for turning small sums of money into a huge fortune, than Russ von Hoelscher. To say that <u>Russ is a genius when it comes to making money is an understatement</u>. He has discovered many different cutting edge strategies and systems over the years, but this new Direct-Mail breakthrough for getting paid up to $73,150.00 for mailing as few as 1,000 sales letters and order forms is his ultimate wealth-making discovery! Thanks, Russ!

(8) Every great wealth-making plan starts with an extremely valuable product or service that is highly in demand. Remember this, as we explain our 'MILLIONAIRE TRAINING PACKAGE.' **The three products and services**

---

in this package are **THE FOUNDATION of our Mailing Co-Op Wealth System** (which is the name of our Affiliate Mailing Program that is designed to pay our Partners up to $73,150.00 for mailing as few as 1,000 Direct-Mail letters). **The first question you must ask yourself when researching any business plan is:** *'What is the products or services behind this opportunity?"* The answer to this question will tell you how solid or weak the plan is. With this in mind, please read closely as we tell you about ALL THREE of the valuable products and services in our 'MILLIONAIRE TRAINING PACKAGE."

(9) We call the 26 strategies in our 'MILLIONAIRE TRAINING Audio Program' (and that we teach in our 2-day '$100-MILLION DOLLAR WORKSHOP) 'The A-to-Z Wealth Formula'... These are the top twenty-six methods that were most responsible for helping us go from $300.00 to over $100,000,000.00 in Direct-Response Marketing sales, in our first 19 years. We love teaching these strategies to other ambitious people. Why? Because we know that **the same methods and strategies that have brought us over one hundred million dollars in total revenue, can make other people as much or even more money than we've made.** I tell you this for good reason: You see, these 26 strategies are an important part of two of the three products and services that are in our 'MILLIONAIRE TRAINING PACKAGE'. They are our greatest way to help people make huge sums of money, even if they are starting with very little.

(10) **School is never out for the pro. The more money you want to make, the more time and money you must put into your education.** You must invest in as many training programs and attend as many seminars and workshops that you can go to. This is one of the biggest secrets to our own success. In fact, we have spent an estimated amount of over ONE MILLION DOLLARS on our own education, to learn all of the secrets we now freely share with our Clients who attend our seminars

and workshops...

(11) Why would someone pay almost $5,000.00 to attend a seminar? That's simple: because they know that **all it takes is a handful of great cutting-edge tips, tricks, and strategies that they can get during these events, to make huge sums of money!** Just a handful of these powerful ideas can turn everything around for them... Just a few of the ideas I have received at some of the seminars (that I have invested thousands of dollars to attend) have been worth millions of dollars to me. My experience is not uncommon. I have spoken to many successful entrepreneurs who have told me that they left a seminar with just one of two ideas (that they didn't have before they came) that instantly made them huge sums of money! Remember this. **It does not matter how much money something costs... The only thing that matters is how much money it makes you... and attending seminars can make people a lot of money!** The more you think about this, the more convinced you will be that our 2-day '$100-MILLION DOLLAR WORKSHOP' is worth every penny of the $3,985.00 price tag.

(12) I am known as *'The Blue Jeans Millionaire'* because I refuse to buy and wear a $5,000.00 suit... I also refuse to wear a tie. **Plus, most importantly; I refuse to try and pretend that I'm something I'm not.** Many people are shocked when they spend a premium price to attend our seminars and find me in blue jeans and tennis shoes... Some people hate this. Others are inspired by it. All I'm trying to do is be myself. I cannot stand people who pretend to be one thing and then do another, and I'm sure you feel the same way. The positive thing about this is the fact that **many people walk away from our seminars with the full realization that if an average person like me can make millions of dollars, then they can do it, too.** I want YOU to have this realization!!! Fully accepting the fact that all the money you want, need, and truly deserve is within your reach, is the first step towards getting rich. If

attending one of our seminars does nothing else for you than giving you this powerful realization, then it will be worth much more than the price you pay to come to Kansas and spend a few days with us.

(13) Do you still think that the regular price for our 2-day '$100-MILLION DOLLAR WORKSHOP' is overly inflated? If so, I don't blame you for being skeptical. But don't let your doubts stop you from checking this out for yourself. **Do a little investigation and you'll find that many people are charging this amount OR EVEN MUCH MORE for similar types of hands-on wealth-making training events.** I don't blame you for being skeptical about this. It's great to have STRONG DOUBTS about everything you read and hear. But a little investigation will prove to you that we are being honest with you about the regular price we have placed on this event.

(14) This third and final item in our valuable 'MILLIONAIRE TRAINING PACKAGE' is the lowest level Distributor position in our revolutionary new Multi-Level Marketing company. However, this is also A GATEWAY POSITION that will (hopefully) lead these new Distributors to wanting to know everything about our Direct-Response Network. The more they know, the more they'll want to know! This can lead to huge sums of money for them and for our 'Affiliate Mailing Partners' who are using the sales letters we provide to offer the M.T.P. to the millions of people who are desperately searching for a way to make more money.

(15) Most of the Clients who were on this conference call are part of the original group of 'Founding Members' of our Direct Response Network. We decided to add the entry level position in our new MLM company as part of this package, in an attempt to help all of our Distributors make more money. There is a lot to learn about this tremendous opportunity. Unfortunately there is not enough room in this book to cover

any of it. But here's the basics: **The Direct-Response Network offers our Distributors a whole new way to make money in MLM without talking to anyone!** We achieve this goal by combining the power of Direct-Response Marketing and the power of Multi-Level Marketing together — and then add FOUR ADDITIONAL MULTI-BILLION DOLLAR MARKETING METHODS to the mix.

(16) Chris is right! The Direct-Response Network is truly a revolutionary new breakthrough for getting rich in MLM without talking to a single person! The people who receive our complete 'MILLIONAIRE TRAINING PACKAGE' will be shocked and amazed when they realize the full extent of what we are giving to them, by providing them with this amazing entry level position!

(17) Our 2-day '$100-MILLION DOLLAR WORKSHOPS' are held on a regular basis, so **all the people who purchase the MILLIONAIRE TRAINING PACKAGE will be able to attend these valuable life-changing events on a date that is perfect for them.** However, we will always make the un-edited recordings available for those who can't or won't take the time to travel to Kansas and attend these events.

(18) **When it comes to explaining THE FULL VALUE of our powerful MILLIONAIRE TRAINING PACKAGE, Chris and I only covered the tip of the iceberg!** The start-up package that goes out to all of our Affiliate Mailing Partners for our new Mailing Co-Op Wealth System goes into much more depth... The important thing for you to remember is this: **The real value of any business opportunity is in the quality of the products and services being sold.** That sounds like common sense, doesn't it? And yet, as Mark Twain said over 100 years ago; "Common sense is a very uncommon thing!" These words are even more true today. So many of the business and money-making opportunities being offered today ARE BUILT ON VERY WEAK FOUNDATIONS. The

products and services sold are either part of some short-term fad or there's no real market for them beyond the base of distributors who peddle them or they are overly inflated and overly hyped. If you want to get rich, you must be very choosy about the types of products and services you promote. Again, this sounds like common sense, but when you see and study all of the junk being sold today, you'll realize that the words of Mark Twain ring even more true today.

(19) If somebody said to me: "Can you please explain your new Direct-Mail secret that gives me the ability to make up to $73,150.00 for mailing 1,000 letters in the shortest period of time?" I'd repeat these words; **"This amazing new business plan consists of a special Distributorship and 3-Level Affiliate Program that lets you and your Affiliate Mailing Partners offer this Millionaire Training Package to the millions of people who are out there desperately searching for a way to make money!"**

(20) The sales letter our Affiliate Mailing Partners use was written by experienced professionals (Chris Lakey and me, T.J. Rohleder) who have a long established track record of selling millions of dollars worth of similar products and services by Direct-Mail. It does a powerful job of offering the complete MILLIONAIRE TRAINING PACKAGE for 89% off the regular price. **This tremendous offer is designed to get THE LARGEST NUMBER of highly qualified prospects to respond now!**

(21) Our 3-level Affiliate Mailing Program is designed to make you up to $73,150.00 or more, for mailing as few as 1,000 letters. However, this is not a guarantee or promise that you will earn this amount or any specific sum of money. Please see our Legal Disclaimer at the beginning of this book. However, having said this, I must also remind you that EVERYTHING WITHIN OUR POWER has been done to help all of our Affiliate Mailing Partners get the largest

percentage of response on every 1,000 Direct-Mail letters they mail. Nobody can ever say for sure exactly how much money anyone will receive on any mailing. There are simply too many variables that affect the percentage of response. **However, because our success is directly tied to our Affiliate Partners' success, we will continue doing everything we can to help all of our Affiliates get the highest percentage of response, just like we do on a daily basis for our own Direct-Mail promotions.**

(22) **The nine items I cover here in some detail are the basis of the Mathematical Income Projections Charts in this book that show you how it's potentially possible to get paid $73,150.00 for mailing 1,000 Direct-Mail letters.** Please read closely. Then study the chart. You'll see, this is very simple to understand. In fact, its simplicity makes it easy for you to quickly come up with your own income projection charts that are based on various percentages of response for each 1,000 Direct-Mail letters that you and your Affiliate Mailing Partners mail.

(23) Not only are we letting all of our Affiliate Mailing Partners sell our complete MILLIONAIRE TRAINING PACKAGE for a full 89% off the regular price, but we are also paying them a full $150.00 commission on each Direct-Mail sale they make! Anyone can say, *"We are doing all they can to help you make the most money."* — BUT WE REALLY ARE DOING IT!

(24) **Our Mathematical Income Projection proves this:** All that our Affiliate Mailers need to potentially get paid $73,150.00 is to mail 1,000 of our Direct-Mail letters and receive an average response rate of 1.1%. This means that 989 out of every 1,000 people who receive the Direct-Mail letters can throw them in the trash and each mailer can still earn this huge sum of money. Amazing!

(25) Your percentage of response in Direct-Mail will always vary, depending on the mailing lists you are using and the specific offer you are making to that list. **The best things you can do to keep your response rate sky high are to:** **A.** Get your mailing lists from the best mailing list brokers you can find. Have them track down the mailing lists of past buyers who have recently bought similar types of products and services that you are selling. **B.** Make sure your Direct-Mail sales letters are written and designed by experts who have been in the business for many years and have a long history of bringing in huge sums of money. **C.** Make sure your sales material makes people an offer that is so irresistible, that they can't say 'NO' and throw it away. These are the three simple steps to making millions of dollars in Direct-Mail... They are also the three steps that we have used to develop this powerful 3-level Affiliate Mailing Program that's designed to pay our Affiliate Mailers up to $73,150.00 or more for mailing as few as 1,000 pieces of Direct-Mail.

(26) This Affiliate Mailing Program is complete. We supply each Mailing Partner with everything they need. PLUS, we make it very easy for each partner to use the same suppliers that we have used for many years to bring in a fortune with our own Direct-Mail promotions.

(27) The greatest thing about this amazing new way to make money in Direct-Mail is the simple fact that you are not only getting paid on your own mailings, but you are also getting a generous percentage on the Direct-Mail sales of your Affiliates, and the Affiliate Mailing Partners they attract through their own mailings. As you'll see; **this LEVERAGE POWER can really add up.** It's similar to rolling a small snowball down a mountain; it just keeps getting bigger and bigger!

(28) Our Mailing Co-Op Wealth System gives our Affiliates the same type of LEVERAGE WEALTH-MAKING POWER

that is normally reserved for the world's richest people. This is an amazing breakthrough — because **each Affiliate Mailing Partner is able to benefit greatly from the combined resources and total Direct-Mail sales of many other Mailing Partners.** Study the lives of the world's richest people and you'll see; these people always have many other things that they make their money on that have little or even nothing to do with their own time, work, and money. They have other people and other things that automatically make money for them. Now this same wealth-making power is available to all of our Affiliate Mailing Partners!

(29) Our Affiliate Mailing Program lets each one of our Mailing Partners cash in from one of the best-kept secrets for getting rich. Here it is: *"You must find a way to make huge sums of money with bad numbers."* In other words, the business plan you choose must let you make a lot of money, even if you do not achieve good results. This is very important. Remember, nobody can accurately predict the future. The meteorologists in Kansas (my home state) cannot even predict what the weather will do! So smart businesspeople do all they can to FIGURE OUT HOW TO MAKE LARGE SUMS OF MONEY — EVEN IF THINGS DON'T WORK OUT THE WAY THEY WANT. This is just one of the most important wealth-making secrets we have built into this amazing Affiliate Mailing Program.

(30) One of my favorite success quotes is: *'Little hinges swing BIG doors!'* Here's why: Sometimes it's the smallest of things that can produce the largest amount of money for all of us. For example, this revolutionary new Direct-Mail wealth-making secret came from a casual conversation with marketing legend; Russ von Hoelscher. If I had not flown in early to San Diego and had supper with Russ, and then had the rather long conversation with him, we would have never discovered this amazing secret. Now listen carefully; I firmly believe that many people will become super rich with this new Affiliate

Mailing Program. That's only my opinion and not a guarantee or promise, but it's based on all the information we covered during our 70-minute presentation and the things I am saying to you right now in this special commentary... Anyway, if I'm right and many people do get super rich — it will ALL have happened because of this small comment that Russ von Hoelscher made to me in the late hours of the evening on March 1st, 2007. **You never know when the perfect wealth-making idea will hit you... This is why you must always associate with the very best people and put yourself in 'the right place' with these highly talented people as often as you can.**

(31) **A 3-Level Affiliate Program simply means that three people get paid a commission each time a product is sold.** Each Affiliate is not only paid on their own sales, but on the future sales of three other people who were introduced to the Distributorship as a direct result of their own individual mailings and the combined mailings from a group of as many as hundreds or perhaps thousands of Affiliate Mailing Partners. (There are many 'two level Affiliate Programs on the Internet. All we have done is added an exciting third level that gives all of our Affiliate Mailing Partners the opportunity to make huge sums of extra automatic cash!)

(32) We have been making money with Direct-Mail since 1988. **We've mailed well over one hundred million pieces of Direct-Mail and have taken in a total of over $100-MILLION DOLLARS.** Now the best of the best of our knowledge, experience and proven track record has gone into this powerful Mailing Co-Op Wealth System. We will work carefully with all of our Affiliate Mailing Partners and do EVERYTHING within our power to help all of them get the highest amount of response on every 1,000 Direct-Mail letters they mail.

(33) The fact that each Affiliate Partner must only mail 1,000

Direct-Mail letters, makes this the most duplicatable wealth-making system I have ever seen in all my years of researching and investigating business and money-making opportunities. **Duplication is the key to wealth.** Remember; nobody gets rich on their own efforts alone. All of the wealthiest people have other things and other people who make money for them. Our powerful Affiliate Mailing Program gives all our Partners the ultimate opportunity to do this in a whole new way.

(34) Any program that claims to have the potential to bring in as much as $73,150.00 for mailing only 1,000 Direct-Mail letters does sound way too good to be true... Because of this, many people will question the legality of such a program. However, **it's very important for you to know that this is legal, for these main reasons:** (1) The products being sold are of the highest quality and sold at an amazing low price. (2) No purchase of the product being sold is necessary to become an Affiliate Mailing Partner. (3) Although we provide a complete Direct-Mail letter and order form (and even offer a service that lets our Affiliate Partners use the same expert suppliers that we use on a daily basis to mail millions of pieces of our own Direct-Mail) — each Affiliate Partner is an independent contractor and free to sell the MILLIONAIRE TRAINING PACKAGE and attract other Affiliate Partners in any way they choose. (4) We have no promise or guarantee that our Partners will earn any specific sum of money. **We have seen many other affiliate programs and distributorship opportunities that fail in each one of these four critical areas.** Now listen closely; I am a very positive person and hate to reflect on the negative.... However, it is very important for you to know that this is an honest, ethical, and legitimate business opportunity in every way.

(35) Mixing a number of different mailing lists together is one of the ways that our expert suppliers can help all of our Affiliate Mailing Partners make the maximum amount of money. **This is one of the BIGGEST SECRETS that all the largest**

Direct-Mail marketers do to limit their risks.... However, most newcomers don't know about this secret or cannot afford to rent multiple mailing lists from various sources so they can mix them. But this is something our experts take care of for all of our Affiliate Partners — for no extra cost.

(36) **Isn't it crazy to sell a product or service without sampling it yourself? I think so.** Most people do, too. This is why most people will want to order the MILLIONAIRE TRAINING PACKAGE, before they decide if they want to participate in the Affiliate Mailing Program. Again, this is just common sense. However, it is our sincerest hope that everyone who orders this package will use it in the fullest way. **We are deeply committed to helping people make money, and there's no better way to do it than with this MILLIONAIRE TRAINING PACKAGE.** We will do our best to give each Affiliate Partner in the greatest training possible, to see to it that they make the largest amount of money.

(37) *CONSIDER THIS:* An opportunity where you and your Affiliate Mailing Partners can each mail 1,000 Direct-Mail letters, and 988 of every 1,000 people can say 'NO' to ordering the package, and you can still potentially get paid $73,150.00 has got to be one of the most powerful opportunities ever!

(38) The most beautiful thing about this simple business plan is the fact that **each Affiliate Mailing Partner must only do a small amount of mailings and get a fairly small percentage of response, to potentially make huge sums of money!** Our simple mathematical income projection chart that is printed throughout this book is the best example to illustrate this. In this mathematical example, all you and your Affiliate Mailing Partners are doing is mailing 1,000 pieces of Direct-Mail. If each Partner does this and averages a little over 1% response, the results are phenomenal! Of course, this is only a

mathematical projection chart, and not a guarantee or promise of actual results, and yet **it does a great job of illustrating the power of this amazing Direct-Mail system that can reward each Affiliate Partner in the greatest way, for only doing a small number of actual mailings.**

(39) Chris is right! You really should grab a calculator and create your own mathematical income projection charts. Do this RIGHT NOW and you'll discover how simple, easy, and highly lucrative this business plan can be. Who says math can't be fun? Go ahead and do this now!

(40) **Mailing your Direct-Mail letters to the very best mailing lists you can get is the most vital part of this entire Affiliate Mailing Program.** The best sales letter will not produce any results if you're mailing it to a bad mailing list. Remember this. We have tested THOUSANDS of mailing lists over the years... Some of these lists have produced massive profits!!! However, some of the lists we've tested (even though we rented them through the best mailing list managers in the nation) completely bombed. In other words, our sales were $0. This is one of the sad realities of this business that you must be aware of. **The way to insure you get a good mailing list is to mail your Direct-Mail letters to a MIXTURE of different mailing lists THAT HAVE BEEN COMBINED TOGETHER, before you mail your Direct-Mail packages to them...** This is one of the main benefits of working with expert suppliers like the ones we introduce to our Affiliate Partners.

(41) **Mailing your sales letters to a combination of mailing lists that have been mixed together is a Direct-Mail wealth-making secret that you won't find anywhere else!** I'm serious. I have invested tens of thousands of dollars on a wide variety of books and programs for making money with Direct-Mail and only found this secret presented a few times. However, as I have tried to explain to you; mixing as many

different individual mailing lists together — so the 1,000 Direct-Mail letters you mail stands the greatest chance of pulling in the highest percentage of response is one of the best things you can do. This will help to insure that you have some really good names on these mailing lists that are mixed with any bad names that may also be on each one of these mailing lists... You minimize your risk and put yourself in the greatest position to make the most money possible.

(42) The fact that all of our Affiliate Mailing Partners are getting the best of the best of the same tips, tricks, powerful strategies, and using the same expert suppliers we have used for many years is one of the most powerful things that we are doing to help them make the largest sum of money!

(43) TOTAL LEVERAGE POWER: **Most people could never afford to mail 132,000 pieces of Direct-Mail.** However, with this Program, if each Affiliate Mailing Partner only mails 1,000 of these Direct-Mail and receives an average response of 1.1% (who also become Affiliate Mailers), then the potential to be making money on a minimum of 132,000 pieces of Direct-Mail is definitely within your reach!

(44) This amazing Direct-Mail breakthrough lets you share in the combined resources of a group of Affiliate Mailing Partners who are working together to help each other make the largest sum of money. **Each Partner only does a small amount... But together, these small amounts add up to give you tremendous money-making power that most people could never afford on their own.** It's simply amazing!

(45) This powerful Affiliate Mailing Program is a true win/win/win situation: **You and your Affiliate Mailing Partners win** because all you are doing is mailing 1,000 Direct-Mail letters and being able to profit from the combined resources of a group of other mailers. **The customers who purchase the MILLIONAIRE TRAINING PACKAGE win,** because

they are getting a valuable combination of three money-making products that are worth $4,529.95, for 89% off the regular price. And these three products are designed to help them make huge sums of money! **And we win**, because we are reaching new customers for our tremendous products and services that we would have never reached without the aid of our Affiliate Mailing Partners. Everyone wins!!! Everyone can make money with this!

(46) Letting people save a full 89% off on this powerful wealth-making package is the ultimate way to help all of our Affiliate Mailing Partners make the largest sum of money... Consider this: Our Affiliates will use our powerful sales material, to sell three products that have a real world value of $4,529.95 — for a full 89% off the regular price. This has got to be one of the greatest offers in history!!! **It's designed to help our Affiliate Mailers make the largest amount of money for mailing the smallest number of Direct-Mail packages.** Here's how: In this day and age of over competition, there are tens of millions of people who suffer from "*information overload.*" — This simply means that they are so bombarded with so many advertising messages and other distractions that the only way to get them to respond to your offer is to make them an offer that is so powerful IT CUTS THROUGH THE CLUTTER AND GETS THEIR ATTENTION AND INTEREST!!!! This is exactly what letting people save 89% off on our valuable MILLIONAIRE TRAINING PACKAGE is designed to do. People will be shocked! And this will help all of our Affiliate Mailing Partners get the highest percentage of response from the letters they mail.

(47) I love the win/win/win nature of this amazing Direct-Mail business opportunity! The more you think about what we have developed, the more you will love it, too! **Most opportunities are 'win/lose' — the promoters are the ones that win and the people using the business opportunity are the ones who lose...** The real exception to this rule are

'franchised business opportunities' where the parent company sets you up with a version of their already tested and proven business model and then does everything possible to help you make the largest amount of money. The more they do to help you, the more money they make. But as you know; franchises can cost tens or even hundreds of thousands of dollars. Some cost millions. But these business opportunities work, because the parent company (the franchisor) does everything possible to help the person who invests in the business opportunities (the franchisee)... The more the franchisee does to help the franchisor, the more money everyone makes.... Now get this: the franchise industry is a ONE TRILLION DOLLAR industry, and although our Affiliate Mailing Program is NOT a franchise, it works along the same lines in this one important area: 'We do EVERYTHING POSSIBLE to help all of our Affiliate Mailing Partners achieve the greatest success possible. The more we can do to help them make the largest amount of money, the more money we make for ourselves. **When you study this opportunity, you'll realize that we are using THE ONE TRILLION DOLLAR WEALTH SECRET of the world's most successful franchises, to do all we can to help our Affiliates make the largest sum of money in the fastest period of time, with the least amount of effort.**

(48) Getting paid $73,150.00 for mailing 1,000 is based on mathematical income projections based on a specific number of Direct-Mail sales, that are made by three levels of Affiliate Mailing Partners. However, having said this, you must also completely understand that we have done and will continue to do everything within our power to help all of our Affiliate Mailing Partners achieve THE HIGHEST PERCENTAGES OF RESPONSE possible on all of the Direct-Mail packages they mail. **The more you study this opportunity, the more you will realize just how we are striving to do all we can to help our mailing partners achieve the highest percentages of response possible.** There are no guarantees or promises,

but thanks to the LEVERAGE WEALTH POWER of this simple business opportunity, it is potentially possible to make huge sums of money, by only mailing a rather small number of Direct-Mail letters!

(49) Our expert suppliers can mail these letters cheaper than you can. These experts (known as 'Mailing Houses') get special postage rates that are out of reach for the average person. This gives you tremendous power! Here's why: **The tremendous postage discounts they pass along will more than cover the fees they charge for their mailing services.** Because of this, you do not actually pay them one penny for their services!

(50) Letting our Affiliate Mailing Partners use the same expert suppliers we use to mail millions of our own Direct-Mail packages, is one of the greatest ways we help them make the largest amount of money. These expert suppliers pass along huge volume discounts for all our partners. They also supply the very best mailing lists (the same lists we use to make money with our own Direct-Mail) and the best postage discounts that are not available to the average person.

(51) Printing our 8-page Direct-Mail sales letter on lightweight newsprint paper saves our Affiliate Mailing Partners a ton of money! This also makes them more money because as the old adage goes; "the more you tell the more you sell!" We have eight pages of selling power that is printed on lightweight newsprint, so your postage rates remain as low as possible

(52) **The fact that there are seasoned professionals who can mail all of your Direct-Mail for you makes it so easy for you to keep mailing more letters!** For best results, you and your Affiliate Mailing Partners should take a percentage of every dollar they bring in and put it back into letting these suppliers mail more Direct-Mail packages for you. This is the secret to making the largest amount of money. We will

encourage all of our Affiliate Mailing Partners to do this and make it as simple and as easy as possible for them to do this. This is designed to help all of our partners make huge sums of long-term cash!

(53) THE NUMBERS DON'T LIE: Although the mathematical income projection charts in this book are just that; 'mathematical' and not a guarantee that you will earn this amount, or any specific sum of money; the numbers still do not lie... For example: **If each Affiliate Mailing Partner only mails 1,000 Direct-Mail packages and then gets an average of 1.1% response (from people who purchase our MILLIONAIRE TRAINING PACKAGE and then also choose to become participating Affiliate Mailing Partners), then you would get paid $73,150.00.** So knowing this, our job is to do all we can to: **#1:** Help each Affiliate Mailing Partner receive the highest percentage of response from the Direct-Mail packages they mail, and **#2:** Make it as easy as possible to mail their 1,000 Direct-Mail letters to the very best mailing lists that are available. Everything we have developed for our Mailing Co-Op Wealth System was done with these two main objectives in mind.

(54) Based on the mathematical income projection charts: if you and your Affiliate Mailing Partners all mailed 1,000 Direct-Mail packages and achieved an average of 1.1% response (of product buyers who also became affiliate mailers and did the same thing), then you would ultimately have a total of 132,000 order forms with your name on them! **Yes, this would give you one hundred and thirty two thousand Direct-Mail packages in the mail that you are scheduled to get paid a commission on! And all you did was mail 1,000 Direct-Mail letters yourself!** Isn't that one of the most exciting things you've ever heard?

(55) Each Affiliate Mailing Partner will receive a complete Start-Up Package that makes is so simple and easy to get started.

But <u>this</u> <u>is</u> <u>just</u> <u>the</u> <u>beginning</u>! **We also work very closely with all our Affiliates and do all we can to help them make the largest amount of money in the minimum amount of time, with the least amount of work.** The more money we can make for all our partners, the more money we make for ourselves, too.

(56) Ask yourself: *"What other business can I get started in for only the cost of mailing 1,000 Direct-Mail packages, that has the potential power to make this kind of money?"* The more you ask yourself this question and think it though, the only answer you'll come up with is: "NONE!"

(57) Most small businesspeople work way too hard, for way too many hours, for way too little pay. The dream of having their own business has now turned into major nightmare. **When you compare this amazing new Direct-Mail business opportunity to all of those businesses, you'll see; this truly is revolutionary!**

(58) This Affiliate Mailing Program has the powerful potential to make huge sums of fast cash! All each Partner has to do is mail 1,000 Direct-Mail packages. Question: How long does that take? Answer: IT CAN HAPPEN VERY QUICKLY. This puts all of our Affiliate Mailing Partners in the position to make the largest sums of money super fast!

(59) Beware of all the people who 'claim' they want to help you get rich. Ask yourself what their motive is. If you can't get a clear answer, then maybe you're being scammed. I'm serious. You must be careful. If the promoters of these opportunities cannot show you A CLEAR SELF SERVING ADVANTAGE on their part to help you make money, then you should be very careful in your dealings with them. So why are we so serious about helping you get rich? *Keep reading…*

---

(60) ***Here's why we want to help you get rich:*** Our 'Mailing Co-Op Wealth System' lets us make more money, by reaching a much wider audience for the three valuable products in our MILLIONAIRE TRAINING PACKAGE. This is our primary reason for doing everything we can to help all of our Affiliate Mailing Partners make the largest sum of money.

(61) If somebody was to ask me, *"What's the most important thing about your Mailing Co-Op Wealth System?"* I'd have to answer by saying: *"It's the fact that we have taken the best-of-the best of all of our knowledge and experience in making over $100,000,000.00 in Direct-Response Marketing sales, and put it into this powerful Program. Then we do everything within our power to help all of our Affiliate Mailing Partners make the largest amount of money."*

(62) We will do everything possible to teach our Affiliate Mailing Partners our ultimate tips, tricks and cutting-edge strategies that have enabled us to generate over $100-million dollars worth of Direct-Response Marketing sales. Our best wealth-making secrets will become their ultimate wealth-making secrets that can potentially help them make even more money! **The more we can do to work with and train all of our Affiliate Mailing Partners, the more they can collectively do to help each other make the largest sum of money.**

(63) The only way somebody can truly be proud of the products and services they're selling is to sample them for themselves. This is one of the most important reasons that we encourage all Affiliate Mailing Partners to purchase and use the products in our MILLIONAIRE TRAINING PACKAGE. It's a well known fact that users of the products make the best salespeople. Using the products and services that are sold in this (or any business opportunity you get involved with in the future), the more you will be doing to increase your chances of making the largest amount of money.

(64) We do let people become Affiliates without purchasing the products. However, **the more they know about this opportunity, the more they will want to buy and use the three valuable items in our MILLIONAIRE TRAINING PACKAGE. Why is this important?** Two reasons: **#1:** The training they receive by using the three products in this package can help them become better Affiliate Mailing Partners and make more money for you! **#2:** You will still be paid your commission if and when these free affiliates do decide to make the purchase! In other words; let's say somebody decides to become an Affiliate Mailing Partner and does not purchase the MILLIONAIRE TRAINING PACKAGE... We will still do everything within our power to help them make the largest sum of money. The more they know about us, and this Program, the more excited they'll be! So a few weeks or months later, if and when they do go ahead and say: *"I must have this MILLIONAIRE TRAINING PACKAGE!"* and send in the money; YOU AND THE OTHER TWO AFFILIATE MAILING PARTNERS WILL STILL BE PAID YOUR COMMISSIONS!!!

(65) Although this amazing opportunity has the potential power to make all of our Affiliate Mailing Partners big money for mailing a small number of Direct-Mail packages, **the secret to getting rich is to put a percentage of every dollar earned, back into more mailings.** This is something we will encourage all of our Affiliate Mailing Partners to do.

(66) If you and your Affiliate Mailing Partners will take a percentage of every dollar you make and put it back into more mailings, the money can keep coming in, keep getting bigger, and never stop!

(67) Our company has a long track record for doing everything we can to help people make money. This has been our business since 1988. **However, we have NEVER had a Program that let us benefit in such a great way for helping our**

Clients, like this one does. This amazing Mailing Co-Op Wealth System is the ultimate way we can help ourselves make huge sums of money, by also doing all we can to help our partners make the largest sum of money.

(68) This Program doesn't stop with mailing 1,000 Direct-Mail packages. We will continue testing new Direct-Mail packages. Then we will give the best of the best of these new offers to all of our Affiliate Mailing Partners, so they can mail them, too. **This is just one of the ways that we will do all we can to help our Affiliates make the largest amount of money over the longest period of time.**

(69) Towards the end of this 70-minute presentation, I did a complete summary of our Mailing Co-Op Wealth System. I did this to try to help our Clients understand just how simple this Program is. It is so simple to understand and easy to use. **But please don't let the simplicity fool you; this powerful new Direct-Mail breakthrough opportunity really does have the awesome power to make you huge sums of never ending cash that can keep getting bigger!** I have done my very best to clearly explain everything to you in the clearest way possible. Please forgive me for my ramblings. I sincerely hope that you have benefited greatly from this small book and will profit greatly in some way from this information. Remember; this book was sold for informational purposes only and not as an inducement for you to join our 3-level Affiliate Program. That's one of the reasons Chris Lakey and I wrote the next Chapter. Please read it at once; As you'll see, we clearly explain how it's potentially possible for you to make millions of dollars by developing your own Affiliate Program that is loosely based on what we have done to create our own. If you're serious about making huge sums of money, you will find this Chapter to be very exciting! Please read it now!

CHAPTER TWO

Two Dozen Wealth-Making Secrets That Can Make You A Millionaire
...In Absolutely No Time Flat!

As you know, our company; Mid-American Opportunity Research Enterprises, Inc. (a.k.a. M.O.R.E. Incorporated) has been helping people make money since 1988. We have seen and studied thousands of different ways for average people to turn small sums of money into a huge fortune. Over the years, we have discovered SOME AMAZING WEALTH SECRETS that let average people turn small sums of money into a huge fortune...

But we firmly believe that this amazing new Affiliate Mailing Program is our ultimate get rich discovery!

Does that sound like hype? Probably. So I thought I'd write this Chapter to give you our top 24 millionaire making secrets and do my best to prove to you that this amazing new discovery lets you make money with all of them. If you're serious about making huge sums of money, you're going to love this Chapter. Please read closely, as I give you the amazing secrets that have the power to make you a millionaire in no time flat!

NOTICE: These 24 'Millionaire Secrets' were taken from the Start-Up Manual that we provide to all of our Affiliate Mailing Partners. They are printed here for your education only — as an example of the basic wealth-making principles behind this Direct-Mail business opportunity — and not intended as an inducement to get the readers of this book to join our Mailing Co-Op Wealth System.

With this said, here are our 24 greatest millionaire secrets:

Millionaire Secret #1 —

How To Pocket Tens Of Thousands Of Dollars... Super Fast!

The secret to making thousands of dollars in the quickest period of time is simple: 1. Just find a proven secret that is making other people thousands of dollars. **2.** Then discover EXACTLY what they are doing to make all of their money. **3.** Then find as many ways as you can to duplicate their success and correct any mistakes they're making. That's it. This is all you do to put huge sums of money in your pocket in the fastest period of time! Sounds simple, doesn't it? Well it is simple! But don't let the simplicity fool you. You see, if one average person can make huge sums of money with some type of business, then you can, too! Remember that. Ideas are transferable. All you have to do to get rich is duplicate the methods that other people are using to get rich... Just do more of whatever they're doing. This simple formula lets you make as much, or even more money than they're making.

This is the secret we use to discover the hottest secrets that make other people very rich! It is the secret that can make you thousands of dollars very quickly — and keep it coming in for the rest of your life!

Our company has been researching business and money-making opportunities since 1988... We look for the best ideas that other people are using to make huge sums of money... This is how we discovered our 'Mailing Co-Op Wealth System.' Remember, this secret was first discovered by Marketing Guru; Russ von Hoelscher. I was in San Diego when Russ von Hoelscher told me about this amazing secret: *"The money just keeps coming in —*

week after week after week!" And *"The money just doesn't stop!"* he said. That's when I knew we were onto something big! You see, **THE BIGGEST WEALTH-MAKING BREAKTHROUGHS we have ever discovered (the ones that produced many millions of dollars in a short period of time) were made by 'keeping my ear to the ground' and talking closely with the movers and shakers like Russ von Hoelscher.** Russ is a MASTER at turning small sums of money into a huge fortune; so when he talks, we listen! His tips, tricks, and strategies have made us huge sums of money over the years... But this new discovery for getting paid up to $73,150.00 for mailing as few as 1,000 Direct-Mail letters is his ultimate money-making breakthrough! Now we have taken the best of the best of Russ's original discovery and added out own powerful techniques based on our many years of experience — to produce the ultimate wealth making program!

Millionaire Secret #2 —

The #1 Reason Why You Can Sit Back And Quickly And Easily Make Tens Of Thousands Of Dollars A Month... Starting Now!

Our 'Mailing Co-Op Wealth System' contains the best-of-the-best of all the methods that we have used to make tens of millions of dollars in Direct-Mail sales. This is the #1 reason this amazing system can make you thousands of dollars a month... starting now! We've taken all of our best secrets and put them into this amazingly simple, but extremely powerful new money-making plan. Although this is no promise that you will make millions of dollars or any specific sum of money or even any money, **it is a major benefit you should carefully consider, <u>that separates this business plan</u> from all the others** (which were developed by people with no knowledge, no experience, and no proven track record of past performance).

Finding a proven way to make money that is based on the same methods that are already making many people rich is the key to getting very rich in a hurry! Remember this! Our new discovery is based on proven methods that have made us millions of dollars... Now we have simply taken the best of everything we have developed over the years and put it into a simple system that gives you the powerful ability to make up to $73,150.00 for mailing 1,000 letters in the shortest period of time! This amazing new business plan consists of a special Distributorship and 3-Level Affiliate Program that lets you and your Affiliate Mailing Partners offer this Millionaire Training Package to the millions of people who are out there desperately searching for a way to make money!

This truly does give you the powerful opportunity to make thousands of dollars in no time flat!

Millionaire Secret #3 —

How To Get Thousands Of Dollars A Day
...Without Lifting A Single Finger!

Our System has been built from the ground floor to pay you huge sums of daily cash — as much as $1,000.00 a day or more — that comes to you super fast! Best of all, if you are letting the same expert suppliers we use to mail and manage all of our Direct-Mail, you do not have to lift a finger! This is THE EXACT OPPOSITE of the amount of money you can make with most of the business opportunities that we research on a daily basis... You see, most opportunities only pay tiny amounts of money that come to you very slowly. It takes forever to get paid! This is one reason many people go broke. They simply don't make enough money fast enough... They become discouraged and quit.

But our 'Mailing Co-Op Wealth System' is different:

This amazing discovery is designed to pay you huge sums of money very quickly! You can get paid giant sums of cash as often as every week!

Here's why this has the power to make you many thousands of dollars within a few short weeks:

A. You are paid HUGE SUMS OF MONEY for all the sales from the Direct-Mail packages that other people mail!

B. You'll never talk to anyone or do any personal selling!

C. The Direct-Mail packages from you and your Affiliate Wealth Partners does all the selling while you get paid the largest amount of cash!

This is designed to let you get paid the <u>maximum</u> amount of cash in the <u>minimum</u> time — with the <u>least</u> amount of effort! Many average people are already making huge sums of money with Direct-Mail! And our 'Mailing Co-Op Wealth System' makes this opportunity even more powerful for you! Now you are not only getting paid on your sales, but you are also getting paid on the Direct-Mail sales of as many as hundreds, or even thousands of other Affiliate Mailing Partners! This is the ultimate wealth-making leverage for you!

Millionaire Secret #4 —

Why We Are <u>Thrilled</u> To Help You Get Rich!

Most opportunities force you to do everything on your own... They take your money — give you a great-sounding business plan, and send you off on your own.

Now you must figure everything out for yourself.

It's like throwing a 5,000 piece jigsaw puzzle on the floor and expecting <u>you</u> to put it all together. You must figure everything out on your own. It is frustrating and confusing. And to make matters even worse — most opportunities have many missing pieces!

Yes, most business opportunities are similar to a 5,000 piece jigsaw puzzle with 1,789 pieces missing!

Is it any wonder why most people fail?

<u>No</u>!

But you won't have this problem...

Remember, we make our biggest profits by doing everything we can to help you make the largest amount of money in the fastest time — with the least amount of effort! **It <u>is</u> <u>in</u> <u>our</u> <u>best</u> <u>interest</u> <u>to</u> <u>see</u> <u>to</u> <u>it</u> <u>that</u> <u>you</u> <u>get</u> <u>paid</u> <u>the</u> <u>largest</u> <u>sum</u> <u>of</u> <u>money</u> <u>right</u> <u>away</u>!** We will do everything we can to help you make a fast fortune.

You will be a valuable member of our team. Our success is tied to your success! ***<u>BUT THAT'S NOT ALL</u>: <u>WE</u> <u>CAN</u> <u>DO</u> <u>EVERYTHING</u> <u>FOR</u> <u>YOU</u> — <u>IF</u> <u>YOU</u> <u>CHOOSE</u>.*** That's right! You will use the same suppliers and experts we use to build and run our multi-million dollar company!

Millionaire Secret #5 —

The 'Onasis Wealth Secret' That Can Make You Tens Of Thousands Of Dollars A Month... *In As Little As 10 Minutes A Day!*

Our 'Mailing Co-Op Wealth System' is a powerful and totally proven way to make huge sums of money! Remember, each Affiliate Partner must only mail 1,000 Direct-Mail letters. The fact that we make is so simple and so easy for people to mail one thousand of our powerful sales letters makes this opportunity <u>the most duplicatable wealth-making system I have ever seen in all my years of researching and investigating business and money-making opportunities</u>. **Duplication is the key to wealth.** Remember; nobody gets rich on their own efforts alone. All of the wealthiest people have other things and other people who make money for them. Our powerful Affiliate Mailing Program gives all our Partners the ultimate opportunity to do this in a whole new way.

This lets you cash in from the secret of the richest people! **In fact, the Greek shipping billionaire, Aristotle Onasis, said:**

> *"The secret to getting wealthy is to know something that <u>nobody</u> else knows."*

He was right! And this is exactly what we have done...

We have taken the crème de la crème of our greatest millionaire-making secrets that we discovered since 1988, and reduced them to a very simple system that you can do in as little as 10 minutes a day.

Yes, all it takes is as little as 10 minutes a day to cash-in with our proven millionaire-making system! Plus, if you're using our suppliers to mail all your Direct-Mail packages each day, it takes absolutely no time, except for the paperwork you must do to pay your taxes and determine what percentage of your income to put back into more mailings. Remember, with our Direct-Response Marketing methods, you are letting other things and materials do all the selling for you... Add this to the fact that your Affiliate Mailing Partners have this same wealth-making power that you have, and you can see why it's more than possible for you to make a fortune in as little as a few minutes a day! Remember, you can do everything by yourself. Or we can do everything for you!

Millionaire Secret #6 —

How This System Lets You Get Paid The Maximum Amount Of Money — In The Minimum Time.

Most business opportunities pay small sums of money over a

slow period of time. How slow? Well, some popular business plans tell you not to expect a profit for 3 to 5 years!

But who wants to wait 3 to 5 years to make a profit?

Not me. I'm sure you don't either!

What you need is a plan that's designed to pay you the largest amount of money — in the fastest time — with the least amount of headaches and hassles! **And this is _exactly_ what our 'Mailing Co-Op Wealth System' is designed to do for you!**

This System is designed to let you get paid thousands of dollars within days from the time our System, and your Affiliate Mailing Partners go to work for you!

This is not a guarantee or promise that you will make thousands of dollars within days — but others have — and you can, too!

One thing is certain: You will be shocked and amazed when you discover how our 'Mailing Co-Op Wealth System' is designed to pay you many thousands of dollars in the fastest time!

✓ You have the power to get paid thousands of dollars within a few short weeks!

✓ You will have our easy system that's so simple a 12-year-old child can understand and use it.

✓ We will be there for you — to do all we can to see to it that you get paid the largest amount of money in the shortest period of time!

Most people are wasting their precious time and energy by trying to make money with opportunities that will never make them rich.

But you can't make this mistake. Here's something you must know...

Life is too short to work hard and then "hope" you will make big money "someday"...

Most small businesspeople work way too hard, for way too many hours, for way too little pay. The dream of having their own business has now turned into major nightmare. **When you compare this amazing new Direct-Mail business opportunity to all of those businesses, you'll see; this truly is revolutionary!** This Affiliate Mailing Program has the powerful potential to make huge sums of fast cash! All each Partner has to do is mail 1,000 Direct-Mail packages. Question: How long does that take? Answer: IT CAN HAPPEN VERY QUICKLY. This puts all of our Affiliate Mailing Partners in the position to make the largest sums of money in as little as 20 to 30 days!

Millionaire Secret #7 —

How We Help You Stay Home, And Get Rich In Total Privacy.

Most opportunities are <u>not</u> private. You must meet and talk to many people <u>every</u> day. You are exposed. You can't do anything in your business without everyone knowing about it.

In fact, with most opportunities, <u>you</u> must let everyone know what you're doing — or you won't make any money. You must approach everyone you meet and try to get them to buy from you. You life is filled with many people who know everything you're doing. You must meet with all these people and try to get them to do business with you. <u>YOU HAVE NO PRIVACY</u>. There is <u>no</u> escape from <u>all</u> the pressures that are closing in on you...

This is how 95% of <u>all</u> business people are forced to live...

**But you won't have <u>any</u> of these headaches
and hassles with our 'Mailing Co-Op Wealth System'!
You'll make money in total privacy!**

**With our System, nobody will what you're doing to make
all of your money! You will be totally free:**

✓ You will <u>never</u> talk with anyone...

✓ You will <u>never</u> personally sell anything to anyone!

✓ You will be in the powerful position that 99% of all other
people can only dream of!

**If the ability to make money in total privacy were the only
advantage of our wealth-making discovery, it would be one of
the greatest ways to stay home and make money.** *<u>But wait,
there's more</u>!*

For starters...

**You can do everything in as little
as 10 minutes a day or less!**

Most business people work way too hard for little money.
They spend many years putting in long hours with endless
frustrations. They end up quitting and become bitter and angry.

I run into people all the time who used to be in business and
now regret every minute of it. They're filled with anger because
all their dreams of becoming financially free have been crushed...

<u>But I've also seen</u>...

> MANY AVERAGE PEOPLE BECOME MILLIONAIRES! <

I've been a business opportunity investigator and

researcher since 1988 and have met many average people who are making more money than most doctors and lawyers can only dream of!

These people are getting rich because they stumbled onto the right opportunity at the right time! Now they're making many hundreds of thousands and even millions, of dollars! But even more important — many of these people are getting rich with very little time or effort! Yes, as amazing as it may sound — it's the absolute truth! In fact...

Whoever said "it's impossible to get rich quick" WAS WRONG!

I have met many people who started with little or even nothing, and became millionaires in a few short years!

The secret to getting very rich with little time and effort is simple: **All you need are the right systems in place.** These systems take time to build — but once they're built — you can kick back and let them make money for you.

IT SOUNDS TOO GOOD TO BE TRUE AND YET IT IS TRUE:

The world's richest people have many systems in place that make them huge sums of wealth! These people can be shopping, sleeping, or on vacation while their "systems" do all the work for them! *Now this same advantage will be working for you!*

You can cash-in from the powerful 'Mailing Co-Op Wealth System' that we have built for you! **We have worked very hard to build this system for you... Now it's ready to go!** You'll be cashing-in from the same system we're using to reach our goal of making millions of dollars with this amazing discovery!

How We Give You The 3 Simple Things You Need To Make Millions Of Dollars!

Many people <u>never</u> get rich because they don't have the right help from the right people. This is especially true when you're first getting started. You must find experts who know how to turn small sums of money into a huge fortune in the fastest time.

**Just find the right people who help you use
the right opportunity and you can get rich fast!**
This was the #1 secret to our rags-to-riches success.
**It made us millions of dollars very quickly.
IT CAN MAKE <u>YOU</u> A FORTUNE, TOO!**

Listen closely. My wife, Eileen, and I had a lot of help support, and guidance from millionaire-making experts such as Russ von Hoelscher, Dan Kennedy, and Bill Glazer. **Thanks to the help Russ von Hoelscher gave us, we made almost $10,000,000.00 in our first four years!** And thanks to other experts such as Dan Kennedy and Alan R. Bechtold, Jeff Gardner, Eric Bechtold, Chris Lakey, Ken Pedersen, Grace Beaman, Michael Penland, Randy Charach, Kent Sayre, Don Bice, Chris and Kim Hollinger, and many others, including my great staff members who are dedicated and loyal, we've brought in over $100-MILLION DOLLARS in less than 19 years!

<u>Please</u> don't <u>think</u> <u>I'm</u> <u>bragging</u> about <u>all</u> <u>our</u> <u>wealth</u>. <u>I'm</u> <u>not</u>. But I am bragging on the fact that having the right help, support, and guidance from the right people has made us multi-millionaires, starting from scratch. It can make a fortune for <u>you</u>, too!

In fact, all you need are 3 things to get rich:

  1. A ROCK-SOLID business opportunity that lets you make a fortune from the combined efforts of hundreds or

thousands of other people, and has very little or even nothing to do with the amount of time and work you directly put into it.

2. The right help, support, and guidance from experts who have already made a great deal of money for others.

3. A marketing system that does <u>all</u> the work for you.

When you have all three of these things, **the question is not;** *"Will you get rich?"* **OH NO! The only question will be,** *"When will you get rich and how rich will you get?"* **BECAUSE YOU <u>WILL</u> GET RICH!**

In fact...

It's only a matter of how much money you'll make and how fast it will come <u>RUSHING</u> to you!

Remember, this proven opportunity! We have made many tens of millions of dollars in Direct-Mail sales... Now we have taken the best-of-the best of all of our knowledge and experience in making over $100,000,000.00 in Direct-Response Marketing sales, and put it into this powerful Program. Then we do everything within our power to help all of our Affiliate Mailing Partners make the largest amount of money. **PLUS, <u>WE</u> <u>CAN</u> <u>DO</u> <u>EVERYTHING</u> <u>FOR</u> <u>YOU</u>!**

Millionaire Secret #9 —

How This System Lets You Get Rich With The '<u>ONE</u> <u>TRILLION</u> <u>DOLLARS</u> A YEAR WEALTH SECRET!'... Starting Now!

Our 'Mailing Co-Op Wealth System' is similar to a high-dollar franchise! How? That's simple, but amazingly powerful; You see, a franchise does everything they can to make sure each one of its location owners bring in the largest sum of money! This makes huge sums of money for both of them. How much money? That's the shocking part... You see, the franchise industry brings in...

ONE TRILLION DOLLARS A YEAR!

The reason this industry brings in one trillion dollars a year is because the parent company does everything they can to help their individual franchisees make the largest sum of money... **Now you will have this same type of wealth-making power working for you!**

Most opportunities have no way to help you make huge sums of money.

Most opportunities leave you out in the cold... They give you great ideas for making money and then force you to do everything on your own... There's nobody to call. There are no support services to fall back on. You must face many obstacles on your path to getting started — and there's nobody to help you get through them...

Is it any wonder why most people fail?

But our 'Mailing Co-Op Wealth System' is different, because...

We will not let you fail!

With this amazing System — we are there for you every step of the way. Remember, we earn our biggest profits by helping you get off to a powerful start. **The more we can do to help you make the most money in the fastest time, with the least effort, the more money we make!**

THIS GIVES US THE ULTIMATE INCENTIVE TO HELP YOU GET OFF TO A POWERFUL START AND MAKE THE MAXIMUM SUM OF FAST CASH!

THIS IS SO GREAT, I MUST SAY IT AGAIN: The more we

can do to help you make fast money — the more money we will make for ourselves!

This is the ultimate way that I can do everything within my power to help you get rich and put large sums of cash in my pocket!

It's the PERFECT win-win situation for you and me! This gives you the greatest way to cash in with 'THE ONE TRILLION DOLLAR WEALTH SECRET!' **Here's how:** (**1**) The products being sold are of the highest quality and sold at an amazing low price. (**2**) No purchase of the product being sold is necessary to become an Affiliate Mailing Partner. (**3**) Although we provide a complete Direct-Mail letter and order form (and even offer a service that lets our Affiliate Partners use the same expert suppliers that we use on a daily basis to mail millions of pieces of our own Direct-Mail) — each Affiliate Partner is an independent contractor and free to sell the MILLIONAIRE TRAINING PACKAGE and attract other Affiliate Partners in any way they choose. (**4**) We have no promise or guarantee that our Partners will earn any specific sum of money. **We have seen many other affiliate programs and distributorship opportunities that fail in each one of these four critical areas.** Now listen closely; I am a very positive person and hate to reflect on the negative.... However, it is very important for you to know that this is an honest, ethical, and legitimate business opportunity in every way. Although this is not a franchise, the more you consider all these four ingredients; you'll see that this has the main benefits these very high-dollar opportunities have.

Millionaire Secret #10 —

3 Rock-Solid Reasons <u>Why</u> This Opportunity Has The Awesome Power To Make You A Millionaire... *In No Time Flat!*

Remember, one of the hottest ways to get rich is to sell very specialized and highly in-demand information... This is <u>exactly</u>

what you'll be getting when you and your Affiliate Mailing Partners will be offering when you use our 'Mailing Co-Op Wealth System'

Here are the three reasons why these items have the power to make you millions of dollars in the fastest period of time:

(1) The basic items you will have control over <u>are</u> complicated.

(2) These items are very specialized and took a great deal of time and expertise to develop by experienced experts who spent many years to develop them. But now they are finished! And now you can cash in with these items!

(3) This gives you all of the advantages that many of the most knowledgeable and experienced experts have — without knowing <u>anything</u> they know! It gives you the ultimate leverage to get paid the largest amount of money in the minimum time!

Please stop and think carefully about these three main advantages... You'll see. This truly does give you the opportunity to make enormous sums of money in the shortest period of time! It's the simple, but proven formula that has been built into this amazing opportunity truly does have the awesome power to make you a millionaire in no time flat!

Millionaire Secret #11 —

How To Turn A Few Thousand Dollars, Into Millions Of Dollars In Only A Few Short Years!

Most business opportunities are too expensive for the average person. **This is a major problem because it forces people to <u>narrow</u> <u>their</u> <u>choices</u>.** For example; most people cannot afford to spend one million dollars to buy a McDonald's restaurant, or invest in high-dollar commercial real estate... or buy large blocks of stock in some high-tech company that is growing by leaps and bounds.

Listen. As you know by now, I am a full-time business opportunity investigator.

But there's one thing I didn't mention...

Here it is... Most of my Clients are <u>not</u> multi-millionaires who have hundreds of thousands of dollars to invest. So I spend 95% of my time researching low-cost business opportunities...

My mission is to discover unique opportunities that can be started for well under $10,000.00 and have the powerful potential to bring in millions every year!

Does that sound unbelievable? It's not.

Does this make you skeptical? It shouldn't.

**You see, there are many people who started
with less than $10,000.00 and ended up
making many millions of dollars and,
in some rare cases, billions of dollars
for their owners! Yes, billions!**

Making billions of dollars starting with almost nothing is truly rare — but there are many well-known examples of average people like you and me who have done it!

My 3 best examples come from the field of personal computers...

Michael Dell started his company "Dell Computers" from his college dorm! His business grew so fast he had to quit school! Now he's a multi-billionaire!

Steve Jobs and his partner, Steve Wozniak, started "Apple Computer" from Steve's garage — <u>and</u> <u>he</u> was living at home with his mom and dad!

And my best story:

✓ **Bill Gates and his partner, Paul Allen,** started the multibillion dollar money machine called "Microsoft" with less than $10,000.00! Bill was forced to drop out of school because business was booming and he knew if he didn't do something dramatic, he would lose a fortune. His father begged him to stay in school and told him he was ruining his life... But we all know how that story turned out!

Sure, these are isolated examples. But these examples have inspired me greatly! I have spent many years studying wealthy people to try to learn their secrets. And there is one thing I must tell you about as we end this Chapter:

Success Leaves Clues!

Please write this quote down and hang it on your wall or refrigerator or mirror.

Here's what it means:

If you want to get very rich — please "model" ordinary people who are already rich. In other words, find a group of average people who have and are getting rich. Discover <u>all</u> of their greatest secrets... Then try very hard to duplicate their exact actions! That's it! You must search for normal people who are making a huge fortune! This is how I developed our powerful new 'Mailing Co-Op Wealth System!' This gives you the amazing secret that you can use to potentially turn a few thousand dollars into millions of dollars a few short years! This is no guarantee or promise that you will make millions of dollars (see our Legal Disclaimer in the beginning of this book) however, the potential power to make a huge fortune is definitely here!

Millionaire Secret #12 —

How Our System Can Put Tens Of Thousands Of Dollars A Month Into Your Bank Account — While You Shop, Sleep, Or Vacation!

Our 'Mailing Co-Op Wealth System' is designed to make you huge sums of money while you shop, sleep, and vacation, because:

➤ Through the combined efforts of all your Affiliate Mailing Partners, you can get paid GIANT COMMISSIONS on huge numbers of sales… without spending any of your own money.

➤ You and all your Affiliate Mailing Partners (which we manage for you) will <u>never</u> have to do any personal selling!

➤ You will be in the powerful position to make huge sums of money — regardless of the number of hours you put in!

This gives you the advantages of the rich:

• The amount of money you can make is <u>not</u> dependent on the number of hours you put in.

• Your marketing system can make you money while <u>you</u> are shopping, sleeping, or on vacation!

• You can spend more time doing the things you love the most and still make huge sums of money.

Add it up. You'll see. These are the amazing ways that our system is designed to make you tens of thousands of dollars a month while you shop, sleep, or are on vacation!

**This lets you do everything part-time —
from the comfort, privacy, and security
of your own home.**

Working from home is a great joy! You spend a lot of time with your family. You have the satisfaction of knowing that you are doing something that few others can do.

But many opportunities cannot be done from home. You must meet with clients, prospects, staff, and suppliers on a daily basis. Your whole life is wrapped up in one meeting after another. You never have the time to do the things you love to do.

Many ambitious people end up making all the money they dreamed of making — but they lose their family in the process.

✓ They work very long hours away from home.

✓ They're always on the road, flying here and there.

✓ The constant travel burns them out and drives a major wedge between them and their spouse.

But these people have no choice! They chose a business opportunity that forces them to be "out in the field" on a daily basis. You cannot afford to do this...

Listen closely. When I am researching a new opportunity I always ask myself one question, *"Can it be done from home?"* If the answer is *"No!"* then I move on! It's not the perfect way to make money if your whole life must be spent away from the people you love.

Millionaire Secret #13 —

10 More Ways Our System Lets You Get Paid GIANT SUMS Of Never-Ending Cash... Right Away!

Our 'Mailing Co-Op Wealth System' lets you make money without having to spend all your time doing all the things that 99% of other businesspeople are <u>forced</u> to do! Everything is done for you!

This lets you stay home and make huge sums of money <u>without</u> any of the headaches and hassles most people are forced to go through.

You'll have 10 powerful ways to make <u>GIANT</u> <u>SUMS</u> of money right now, without any of the headaches and hassles that most other business people are forced to go through!

Here they are:

1. NO employees
2. NO storefront
3. NO daily commute
4. NO long hours
5. NO overhead expenses
6. NO meetings!
7. NO personal selling
8. NO shipping of products
9. NO contact with others <u>unless</u> you want it!
10. NONE of the headaches most people are forced to go through!

Does all this sound too good to be true?

Well, it is for the average person!

But it's <u>not</u> for you!

All you did was choose a home-based business that was not dependent upon...

✓ **A local market**

✓ **Personal selling**

✓ **Fulfillment and customer service**

Please listen carefully... Most people go into business for themselves in the most unconscious way. They <u>never</u> think it through. They put very little thought in choosing the <u>right</u> opportunity that is perfectly suited for the life they want to live.

<u>YOU</u> <u>CANNOT</u> <u>MAKE</u> <u>THIS</u> <u>MISTAKE</u>.
The business you choose <u>must</u> be custom-built
around the perfect life you want to live.

You must build your business around your ideal lifestyle. You don't want to build your life around your business.

Your business must serve <u>you</u> rather than you serving it. Most people will <u>never</u> figure this out. They choose the wrong business and now their whole life is a living nightmare.

Now they are working way too many hours for too little pay.

Now they are forced to do many things for money that they <u>hate</u> doing. This makes me so sad.

And you will NEVER worry about making this mistake!

Our 'Mailing Co-Op Wealth System' is <u>not</u> dependent on the number of hours you work — or the activities you are <u>directly</u> involved with on a daily basis. These opportunities <u>are</u> <u>rare</u> — but they do exist! In fact, you have one here!

Millionaire Secret #14 —

How to stay home — watch your favorite TV programs — enjoy time with the people you love — catch all the cat-naps you want... *and <u>still</u> get super rich!*

This entire System has been built from the ground floor to be done entirely from home!

You will never have to leave your home to cash in big with our powerful 'Mailing Co-Op Wealth System'! You can stay home each day and enjoy the time with your family — and still make huge sums of money! The only time you'll <u>ever</u> leave home is to deposit the money into your bank. And you don't even have to do that — <u>unless</u> you want!

Yes, you can always mail in your bank deposits if you want!

Being able to make huge sums of money <u>without</u> leaving your home is one of the most thrilling things about our 'Mailing Co-Op Wealth System!' This is such an exciting way to make money!

Consider this... While almost all of your neighbors are forced to jump in their car every day and put up with all the hassles of driving through thick traffic to go to a job they hate, you can be making GIANT sums of money from the comfort of your own home! You can watch them drive away in a mad hurry to get to work every day while you relax at the kitchen table with the morning newspaper and a hot cup of coffee!

You can stay home all day — watch your favorite TV programs — enjoy time with the people you love — and catch all the cat naps you want — and still make a fortune!

Does all this sound like a great fantasy to you?

Something you can only dream of?

Well it's not!

**There are many people living like this every day
of the week right now...** *and YOU can be one of them!*

These people are staying home each and every day — relaxing around the house — and <u>still</u> making a fortune!

One of my best friends loves to get up early each morning just to watch all of his neighbors scramble to work! Some of these people leave every morning when it's still dark and do not get back home until it's dark. They have no time at all for their family and friends. They're killing themselves a little more every day because they hate their job and they hate all the headaches and hassles of traveling to work each day — but they are forced to do it.

You will never have that problem every again: **Our 'Mailing Co-Op Wealth System' lets you stay home and relax and <u>still</u> make more money than most people will make working long hours in some unhealthy office environment!** This one advantage alone is enough of a reason for you to jump for joy because you have the courage and vision to invest in this revolutionary moneymaker!

Millionaire Secret #15 —

3 Powerful Reasons Why You Can Get Paid up to $73,150.00 Or More, Every Time You Drop 1,000 Letters In the Mail.

Remember, the 'Mailing Co-Op Wealth System' secret that gives you the amazing power to make up to $73,150.00 for mailing 1,000 letters is fairly new.

<u>But the foundation behind this amazing wealth system is</u>

<u>not</u> <u>new</u>.

We have been using Direct-Mail since 1989 to bring in many tens of millions of dollars. Here are THREE MORE REASONS why our proven system could be worth <u>millions</u> of dollars to you and your family. Think carefully about all this. These are the three reasons why you can get paid up to $73,150.00 or more, anytime and every time you want to drop 1,000 letters in the mail:

1. Your income comes from the sale of the high-dollar, high-profit products and services that are made by the Direct-Mail packages that you and all of your Affiliate Mailing Partners mail. Remember, this amazing system lets you make money through the combined Direct-Mail packages that are mailed by you and by all of your Affiliate Mailing Partners. This puts you in the powerful position to get paid GIANT COMMISSIONS on huge numbers of sales... without spending any of your own money.

2. The Direct-Mail sales material, our proven methods, and our expertly trained staff, and all of your Affiliate Mailing Partners do the selling for you! Because of this, You and all your Affiliate Mailing Partners (which we manage for you) will <u>never</u> have to do any personal selling!

3. And you also have the amazing opportunity to get paid from as many as hundreds or even thousands of other people who can also be using the same exact 100% duplicatable system that <u>you</u> are using to make all of your money! This puts you in the powerful position to make huge sums of money — regardless of the number of hours you put in!

Our company has a long track record for doing everything we can to help people make money. This has been our business since 1988. **However, we have NEVER had a Program that let us** benefit in such a great way for helping our Clients, like this one **does.** This amazing Mailing Co-Op Wealth System is the ultimate way we can help ourselves make huge sums of money, by also doing all we can to help our partners make the largest sum of money. We will do everything possible to teach our Affiliate Mailing Partners our ultimate tips, tricks and cutting-edge strategies that have enabled us to generate over $100-million dollars worth of Direct-Response Marketing sales. Our best wealth-making secrets will become their ultimate wealth-making secrets that can potentially help them make even more money! **The more we can do to work with and train all of our Affiliate Mailing Partners, the more they can collectively do to help each other make the largest sum of money.**

Millionaire Secret #16 —

How This Amazing System Could Make You A Huge Fortune — For The Next 2 to 3 Decades... And Beyond!

With our System, you will never talk with a single person, unless you want.

All of the other people who are making thousands a month with this basic secret are doing way too much personal selling.

I hate this!

My company is involved in an area of marketing called: "Direct-Response." This powerful form of marketing is responsible for the sale of over 300 billion dollars worth of goods and services each year without any personal selling!

This is the most powerful marketing method on earth! And this is the form of marketing in our revolutionary new Mailing Co-Op Wealth System!

Direct-Response Marketing does an amazing job of selling because...

1. It attracts all of the <u>right</u> people and repels the wrong ones.

2. It brings all of these people to you automatically!

3. It does a powerful job of educating these people on all the major advantages of your product or service.

4. It eliminates <u>all</u> of their biggest objections...

5. Then it makes them want to buy <u>now</u>!

And best of all, it does all of this without any direct effort on your part!

The sales materials and methods we have built into our 'Mailing Co-Op Wealth System' do all the actual selling for you!

These sales materials were designed and built by knowledgeable people who have a long and proven track record for making millions of dollars! They are designed to crank out huge sums of money for you like a well-oiled money machine!

This System gives you such a powerful advantage over all of the other people who are depending on their own marketing efforts to make money! Those people have little or no leverage. But our Mailing Co-Op Wealth System is totally different! This gives our Affiliates the same type of LEVERAGE WEALTH-MAKING POWER that is normally reserved for the world's richest people. This is an amazing breakthrough — because **each Affiliate Mailing Partner is able to benefit greatly from the combined resources and total Direct-Mail sales of many other Mailing Partners.** Study the lives of the world's richest people and you'll see; these people always have many other things that they make their money on that have little or even nothing to do with their own time, work, and money. They have other people and other things that automatically make money for them. Now this same wealth-making power is available to you!

Our company and your Affiliate Mailing Partners will be there for you — to help you make the largest sum of money possible with our powerful marketing system that has been proven to generate many tens of millions of dollars!

Remember, one of the main reasons I am so <u>thrilled</u> about this 'Mailing Co-Op Wealth System' is because of the simple, but powerful, fact that <u>our success is directly tied to your success</u>! The more we do to help you make the largest sum of money in the shortest period of time — the more money we will also be making for ourselves. The fact that our success is <u>directly</u> tied to your success is the most powerful benefit that has been built into our amazing 'Mailing Co-Op Wealth System.'

This gives you the main advantages you would expect from a high-dollar franchise opportunity <u>without</u> spending tens or hundreds of thousands of dollars!

Our 'Mailing Co-Op Wealth System' is not a franchise. But it does give you some of the most beneficial wealth-making advantages.

In fact, the more I think about this, the more I believe that...

Our 'Mailing Co-Op Wealth System' is far <u>better</u> and way more powerful than many franchises that sell for up to $500,000.00 or more!

Okay, that's a bold statement and it's only my strong opinion. But when you go over <u>all</u> of the rock-solid reasons <u>why</u> I firmly believe this, I'm betting **you will be as convinced as I am that in** many ways, this 'Mailing Co-Op Wealth System' beats every other opportunity — including those which cost as much as $500,000.00 or even <u>more</u> to start.

That's a very bold statement. But like everything else I have told you in this manual — I will back it up with <u>solid</u> facts that you can sink your teeth into.

This a long-term opportunity that can make you super rich!

Our 'Mailing Co-Op Wealth System' is designed to make you ever-growing amounts of money for the next 10... 20... and even 30 years and beyond! This can be a part of your estate and all the automatic income you can make is available to your family.

Remember, this revolutionary wealth-making opportunity is a powerful combination of 3 of the hottest multi-billion dollar trends. They are producing billions of dollars right now and <u>the best years</u> are still ahead! Yes, the future is so bright you gotta wear shades!

Listen closely. Although there are <u>no</u> guarantees or promises...

**I firmly believe this opportunity
stands a greater chance of making you
many tens of thousands of dollars month
for the next 2 or 3 decades than
<u>any</u> <u>other</u> opportunity I have ever seen.**

The reason I believe this opportunity can be making you and your family huge sums of money for the next 20 to 30 years and beyond is because of <u>all</u> the reasons we have talked about <u>added</u> together! **If you have been reading this book — you know:** There are so many different powerful wealth-making ingredients that have gone into this revolutionary 'Mailing Co-Op Wealth System!'

It is the explosive combination of all of them working together that has the awesome power to make you massive sums of money for many years!

My favorite combination that creates this synergistic power is...

1. The explosive markets behind this new wealth-maker!

2. The fact that YOU get paid the largest amount of money and not the company who developed this opportunity.

3. The fact that we get paid the largest amount of money for doing everything within our power to help you get paid the largest amount of money in the fastest period of time!

4. The fact that we will manage all of your Affiliate Mailing Partners and do all we can to help them help you make the largest sum of money!

5. The fact that we will continue to develop NEW and MORE POWERFUL Direct-Mail packages that you and all your Affiliate Mailing Partners can mail in the future! This alone has the awesome power to potentially make you huge sums of money for the next 2 to 3 decades and beyond!

When you mix these powerful ingredients together, you create a true money-making explosion that can give you financial independence for the rest of your life!!!

Millionaire Secret #17 —

Why The Money Can Keep Coming To You And NEVER STOP — Even If You Never Mail Another Direct-Mail Letter!

Remember, the amount of money you can get paid has nothing

to do with the amount of actual time you put in!

Because of this, it is possible...

*For you to get paid many thousands of dollars
a month for doing very little of anything!
It's our powerful and proven System that
does all the work for you!*

Our powerful proven system is designed to:

1. Attract the people who are most likely to buy all of the high-profit products and services and/or become your Affiliate Mailing Partners who will be spending their money to help you make money.

2. Make all the sales for you automatically.

3. And then pay you huge sums of money for each high-profit transaction that is done for you!

These things are designed to make you a never-ending stream of steady cash — even if you eventually stop mailing any more Direct-Mail letters!

Yes, this system is designed to do it <u>all</u> for you!

**Remember, you will be cashing-in
with the same powerful marketing methods
that have brought us tens of millions
of automatic dollars!**

We have worked very hard since the mid 1980's to perfect our Direct-Response Marketing skills and abilities. You will be cashing in from our many years of hard work! Our System does <u>all</u> of this for you! This powerful system is the closest thing to an actual money machine you will ever find.

We have worked hard to build this system to make you and all of our Affiliate Mailing Partners, and us, the largest sum of money! This is very important... You'll be plugging into the same exact system we have built to make millions with this amazing discovery! This gives you tremendous power to make massive profits! You will gain leverage from all of our hard work. You'll have the full power of our many years of wealth-making know-how!

We have a long and successful track record for generating millions of dollars from people who we never meet and even talk with!

Not to brag, but we have taken in almost $100,000,000.00 in our first 17 years from our headquarters in rural Kansas. I challenge you to find Goessel, Kansas, on a map! **Here we are in the middle of nowhere — bringing in many millions of dollars a year — with the same system you'll be cashing in with!**

There is no better testament to the money-making power of our amazing Direct-Response Marketing methods! And when you mix our powerful millionaire-making secrets — along with the leverage power of hundreds or even thousands of Affiliate Mailing Partners who will be spending their money to help you make money, and you truly have one of the greatest wealth-making opportunities in history!

Millionaire Secret #18 —

How To Mail A Small Batch Of Direct-Mail Letters Each Month — And Be Set For Life!

Again, at the risk of sounding like pure hype, this is the easiest wealth-making opportunity to start and run that I have ever seen! How easy? That's the shocking part... **You see, there is only one** basic step for you to take; 'mailing your 1,000 sales letters on a regular basis or letting our experts do it for you'. That's it! Just one very simple and easy step is all it takes to set our money-making machine into motion and can make you set for life!

Think of this easy step as a domino. You simply tip it and knock down a whole line of other dominoes that are in front of it...

This is a good visual. Why? You see, it does take a couple of days to understand everything about this opportunity... There are many things you must know <u>before</u> you can simply tip the one domino and watch all of the others fall down!

Of course, 'THIS SINGLE DOMINO' is only a metaphor to try to illustrate the incredible power behind our 'Mailing Co-Op Wealth System.' But it's the most powerful visual example!

Now try to imagine a huge pile of 10,000 dominoes...

Let's say that each one of these dominoes represents a key money-making benefit and advantage that has gone into our powerful 'Mailing Co-Op Wealth System'... <u>You</u> <u>stack</u> <u>them</u> <u>up</u> in a <u>straight</u> <u>line</u>. Then when you get to the end — you have one last domino in your hand.

This final domino is yours alone.

You take this last domino and place in front of the other 9,999. Now you have 10,000 dominoes all stacked up on a huge 100-yard football field or basketball court...

Now all you have to do is tip the first domino and all of the rest of the dominoes will automatically tip over!

This is the best metaphor I can give you to help you

understand the awesome power of our 'Mailing Co-Op Wealth System'! Here's how...

This book tells you a great deal about the
powerful ingredients that are built into this
'Mailing Co-Op Wealth System' so you will fully understand
how all of this is designed to make you a fortune.

But all you need to do is mail your 1,000 sales letters or let our experts do it for you, to set your money-machine into motion!

What's so great about this one basic step?

That's simple, but amazingly powerful!

This step is designed to create a powerful chain reaction that causes huge sums of money to come flowing to you! I can't wait to reveal all of the secrets to you!

Millionaire Secret #19 —

How To Let Up To Thousands Of People Make Money For You... While You Sit Back And Relax!

Our 'Mailing Co-Op Wealth System' gives you the ultimate way to let up to hundreds, or perhaps thousands of other people make money for you!

These Affiliate Mailing Partners (who we manage for you) can use the same powerful ONE-STEP Marketing System that we have built for you. The more you stop and think about this, the more you'll come to appreciate how this is designed to make you a fortune!

When you completely understand everything that has gone into this powerful 'Mailing Co-Op Wealth System', you will be speechless! This really is the most powerful home-based wealth-maker in the world.

Why? Well, when it all boils down to one major advantage:

They give you the same advantages the world's richest people enjoy!

CONSIDER THIS: The world's richest people make money on <u>many</u> things that have nothing to do with the amount of time and work they actually do. They make money from the efforts of other people, from the sale of certain products or services, or from other income producing assets that let them sit back and let their money make more money for them.

Yes, these wealthy people have many ways to continue to earn a fortune, even when they do nothing. Now you can enjoy these same powerful advantages.

Millionaire Secret #20 —

How This Amazing New System Lets You Cash-In From The Wealth-Making Power Of Passive Income... Right Now!

As I am about to show you, there are only 3 ways to make money.

Here they are:

MONEY-MAKING METHOD #1:

You can sell your time for money.

This is the way 99% of the people make almost all of their money. Everyone from day laborers who slave under the hot sun for minimum wage, to brain surgeons who get paid thousands of dollars an hour. All of these people are selling their time for money.

MONEY-MAKING METHOD #2:

**You can sell a product or service
or combination of both.**

With this second method, your money comes from the sale of some product or service, <u>not</u> the amount of time you work. **This is a much smarter way to make money!** In fact, the world is filled with many millionaires who make almost all of their money with this second powerful method.

But the real secret to getting rich is to use the final method.

Just look...

MONEY-MAKING METHOD #3:

**PASSIVE INCOME! You use your money
to make you even more money!**

The 2nd money-making method is quite capable of making you very rich. **But the third method of making money has made more people wealthy than the other two combined!** With this final method, you are putting your money into income-producing assets that automatically make you more money... All you do is sit back and cash the checks you receive for all of your investments!

Now for the best part; our 'Mailing Co-Op Wealth System' lets you cash in with this second and third powerful way to make money! This makes the next secret possible. Read on...

Millionaire Secret #21 —

How Our System Is Built To Let You Make Up To $1,000 A Day — Or A Whole Lot More — <u>Without</u> Doing Any Work!

Our 'Mailing Co-Op Wealth System' is one of the most

powerful ways to make money in the entire world, because ALL the money you can make will come from the methods that are responsible for the GIANT fortunes of the world's richest people.

This gives you the ultimate way to cash-in with the same methods that all of the world's richest people use to make their fortune! The amount of money you can earn has nothing to do with the amount of actual time and work you put in.

And this leads to the biggest benefit of all...

**Because we can run all of this for you —
it is possible for you to make tens of thousands of dollars
a month without doing any work!**

Of course, there are no promises and guarantees that you will make $1,000.00 a day or any specific sum of money for doing absolutely no work — but the potential to get paid many thousands of dollars for letting us run everything for you is definitely here.

Here's why:

1. Your income comes from the sale of the high-dollar, high-profit products and services that are made by the Direct-Mail packages that you and all of your Affiliate Mailing Partners mail.

2. The sales material, our proven methods, and our expertly trained staff do all the selling for you!

3. And you also have the amazing opportunity to get paid from as many as hundreds or even thousands of other people who can also be using the same exact 100% duplicatable system that you are using to make all of your money!

This gives you the power to make up to $1,000.00 a day or more without doing any work!

How We Help You CASH-IN
From The Amazing
ONE BILLION DOLLAR A DAY SECRET!

But wait! Maybe you're asking yourself; *"If this is a method that's making many people like you and your wife instant millionaires, why do you say it is a 'little-known' method?"*

The answer is simple: You see, many people are interested in getting rich in Direct-Response Marketing. This is one of the most exciting ways to make money! And many people fall in love with the idea of getting rich with this powerful form of marketing.

But as I told you, this method of marketing is deceptive.

You see, on the surface it sounds simple, and when you have all the elements working together in the right way, it really is!

However, there are <u>many</u> different details that must be understood and mastered <u>if</u> you want to make millions of dollars in the shortest period of time. Many people don't want to put in the time and work to study and master the more advanced features of Direct-Response Marketing. They go into this half-cocked and do not experience the results they want. Then they quit, and move onto something else.

I'll go into a few of the complexities of this powerful wealth-building method in a moment. And if you pay close attention, and spend some time understanding these challenges and face them head-on, you really can become a millionaire in no time flat!

But first, let's talk about the good things...

Here's the 5 main reasons why this method of marketing can put millions of dollars in your bank account in a few

short years:

1. This proven method is responsible for almost <u>one</u> billion dollars in sales each day!

2. This powerful method of marketing lets you sell to millions of people with <u>no</u> rejection!

3. There is little or even <u>no</u> risk, if you do it right!

4. You can make millions of dollars from the comfort and privacy of your home!

5. When done correctly, a good Direct-Response Marketing System is <u>less</u> like a business, and <u>more</u> similar to a well-oiled money machine!

The Direct-Response Marketing Association says that almost 300 billion dollars are being generated each year through this powerful marketing method. Personally, I believe they are being way too conservative. I believe the "real" number is over <u>twice</u> that amount.

But what difference does it make if it's one or two billion dollars a day? The point is: <u>This</u> <u>proven</u> <u>wealth-making</u> <u>method</u> is making a fortune for tens of thousands of individuals and companies <u>right</u> <u>now</u>! It's like a giant safe that's filled with millions of dollars... All you gotta do is know the combination on the lock and all the money inside is yours!

Now listen carefully. Many people want to make millions of dollars in the fastest time, and that's great... But these people <u>never</u> stop to realize that all the money they want to make is out there right now! This is true for you, too!

Yes, all the money you want to make is waiting for <u>you</u> right now!

Where is this money?

That's simple: It's in the pockets, purses, and bank accounts and credit card limits of tens of millions of people! All you have to do is use the power of Direct-Response Marketing to offer them something that's worth far <u>more</u> money than the sum you are asking for, and they will gladly give this money to you!

This is great news for you!

Why?

Because our powerful ONE-STEP Marketing System is designed to give hundreds of millions of people something that is far more valuable than the amount of money you're asking for in return! By the time you go through this book carefully and think about this very carefully, you'll know <u>exactly</u> <u>why</u> this simple system has the awesome potential to make you a millionaire in no time flat!

Millionaire Secret #23 —

FOUR AMAZING WAYS Our Proven System Is Designed To Let You Relax And Get Paid Many Thousands Of Dollars In Pure Automatic Income For <u>All</u> The Work That Other People Do For You!

Here are the four powerful ways that this system is designed to make you a fortune in pure automatic income:

(1) There is only one basic step for you to do. The other steps are automatically done for you! Plus, as you'll see, the same supplies we depend on to build our multi-million dollar business, as well as our staff, can take care of everything for you!

(2) This one step is simple to understand and easy to use.

In fact, it's so simple and easy a 12-year-old child could quickly understand and use it!

(3) You will either do the <u>ONE</u> step by yourself or let our expert suppliers do it for you. Either way, this automatically sets the other steps in motion! (I like to think of this as a set of dominoes that are all lined up. You simply push the first one and all the others quickly fall down!)

(4) This is designed to make you many thousands of dollars in automatic income! You will <u>never</u> speak with anyone. You will <u>never</u> attend any meetings or pep rallies. (Although we encourage you to get our wealth-making training in our MILLIONAIRE TRAINING PACKAGE, that's designed to help you and your Affiliate Mailing Partners make the maximum amount of money in the minimum time!) All the actual work and selling is done for you by our company, our expert suppliers, and as many as hundreds and perhaps thousands of other people who we manage for you!

If you're like me, it will take you awhile to fully grasp this... However, once you do, you'll see that our system is designed to make it super easy for as many as hundreds or thousands of other people to duplicate the same basic ONE STEP you are using and make you huge sums of automatic money!

Millionaire Secret #24 —

How Our Company, And Thousands Of Other People Can Get Massive Sums Of Never-Ending Cash Coming <u>Directly</u> To You Every Single Week!

This is the most brilliant wealth-making system I have <u>ever</u> seen in all my years of researching business and money-making opportunities! Once you fully understand how this is designed to help you make a fortune, you will be more excited than you have been for years!

I don't blame you for being skeptical about all of this in the beginning. But remember, **a 3-Level Affiliate Program simply means that three people get paid a commission each time a product is sold.** Each Affiliate is not only paid on their own sales, but on the future sales of three other people who were introduced to the Distributorship as a direct result of their own individual mailings and the combined mailings from a group of as many as hundreds or perhaps thousands of Affiliate Mailing Partners. (There are many 'two level Affiliate Programs on the Internet. All we have done is added an exciting third level that gives all of our Affiliate Mailing Partners the opportunity to make huge sums of extra automatic cash!)

The most beautiful thing about this simple business plan is the fact that **each Affiliate Mailing Partner must only do a small amount of mailings and get a fairly small percentage of response, to potentially make huge sums of money!** Our simple mathematical income projection chart that is printed throughout this book is the best example to illustrate this. In this mathematical example, all you and your Affiliate Mailing Partners are doing is mailing 1,000 pieces of Direct-Mail. If each Partner does this and averages a little over 1% response, the results are phenomenal! Of course, this is only a mathematical projection chart, and not a guarantee or promise of actual results, and yet **it does a great job of illustrating the power of this amazing Direct-Mail system that can reward each Affiliate Partner in the greatest way, for only doing a small number of actual mailings.**

This powerful Affiliate Mailing Program is a true win/win/win situation; **You and your Affiliate Mailing Partners win**, because all you are doing is mailing 1,000 Direct-Mail letters and being able to profit from the combined resources of a group of other mailers. **The customers who purchase the MILLIONAIRE TRAINING PACKAGE win**, because they are getting a valuable combination of three money-making products that are worth $4,529.95, for 89% off the regular price. And these three products are designed to help them make huge sums of money! **And we win**, because we are reaching new customers for our tremendous products and services that we would have never reached without the aid of our Affiliate Mailing Partners. Everyone wins!!! Everyone can make money with this!

    And speaking of money, the last Chapter shows you how you could potentially make millions of dollars by developing your own 3-Level Affiliate Mailing Program. This is easier than you may think! Why would I freely share these powerful wealth-making secrets that let YOU get rich, the same way we plan to bring in tens of millions of dollars for ourselves and all of our Affiliate Mailing Partners? That's a great question! Please go onto the next Chapter RIGHT NOW, to discover the answer.

CHAPTER THREE

How to Make Millions With Your Very Own 3-Tier Affiliate Mailing Program!

This Chapter gives you the essential elements you need to develop your own 3-Tier Affiliate Mailing Program. Read closely. As you'll see, this information has the potential power to make you millions of dollars.

Why would we freely give you our best ideas of how you can set up and operate your own 3-Tier Affiliate Mailing Program?

Actually, there are four reasons:

a. This book was sold for informational purposes and not as an inducement to get people to join our own Mailing Co-Op Wealth System. Because of this, it would be incomplete without some very detailed information of how you can potentially make huge sums of money by setting up and running your own 3-level Affiliate Mailing Program.

b. The market is so big that there is plenty of room for competitors, so we're not afraid to share our best ideas with you and tell you <u>exactly</u> what you need to do to duplicate our successful affiliate program. To give your Affiliate Program three levels, you can model it closely after ours. Feel free to sign up as an Affiliate of our Program, and use our ideas to help you create your own program. However, you cannot plagiarize by borrowing too liberally from our own materials, or we'll be forced to take legal action to protect our intellectual property. Remember, ideas themselves are not copyrightable. But if you borrow too liberally from someone's ideas, they can prosecute you for plagiarism.

c. If you put together your own successful affiliate mailing program and it does not directly compete with ours, we may want to become one of your 'master affiliates' and offer your program to our own Affiliate Mailing Partners.

d. The more you investigate what it takes to develop your own Affiliate Program, you will find that it is not that difficult to do. In other words, we are more than happy to share our best secrets with you, because developing your own Affiliate Program is actually quite simple, and you could eventually figure it out on your own.

How simple is this? The answer is shocking!

You see, there are only 5 ingredients you need to develop your own highly successful Affiliate Mailing Program, and have it up and running within a matter of months.

Here they are:

Ingredient #1: A valuable proprietary-based product or service.

Ingredient #2: An irresistible offer to sell your product or service.

Ingredient #3: Powerful sales materials that your Affiliates can use to sell your product or service.

Ingredient #4: The most perfectly targeted mailing lists money can buy.

Ingredient #5: The highest quality Affiliate Support Services you can provide to your Affiliate Partners.

These are the 5 things you need to develop your own powerful Affiliate Mailing Program. I'll spend the rest of this Chapter going over these key ingredients and tell you why they are vital to your success. *So let's begin...*

Ingredient #1:

A valuable proprietary-based product or service.

A valuable product or service is THE ROCK-SOLID FOUNDATION of every successful Affiliate Program. Here are 5 things your product or service must have:

A) **It must be proprietary.** Your product or service must be one that you have either developed yourself or have the exclusive rights to. If people can purchase your product service from a variety of other sources, it makes it more difficult to attract Affiliates who will want to sell it. For example; our 'Millionaire Training Package' is a combination of three 100% proprietary products and services that we have developed ourselves. This lets us control the costs and completely separate our products from similar products and services that others are selling. Your own affiliate mailing program must have this, too.

B) **It must be highly unique.** Your product or service must offer the same types of benefits of that other hot-selling items offer. However it must also be uniquely different. This seems like a paradox, but it's not. Here's why: First, it must be similar enough to other items that are already selling well, so there's an established market for it and you don't have to educate the people in the marketplace of the benefits. But it must also be unique enough that these people will want to buy your product or service instead of what's already available. The more you can do this, the more you'll be putting your Affiliates (and you) in the position to make the largest number of sales.

C) **It must have a huge perceived value.** Your product or service must have a perceived value that is much higher than the price your Affiliates are asking people to give in exchange. This perceived value must be based in reality, not fantasy. For example, we claim that our 'Millionaire Training Package' has a full value of $4,529.95, because it is based on products and services that have and are being sold for that much money or more. Any skeptical prospect can quickly find out that people are selling similar Seminars for $3,000.00 to $5,000.00 each. Therefore, the $495.00 that our Affiliates charge seems pale by comparison to the high perceived value. The product or service that the affiliates for your own program sell must offer this same benefit.

D) **It must be highly in-demand.** There must already be an established market for the types of products and services your affiliates will be selling. To use our 'Millionaire Training Package' as example again, there is a huge demand for Seminars and Workshops that teach people how to make more money, be more successful, sell more products, etc. Our 'Millionaire Training Package' was produced to fill this huge demand. Your products or services must fill an established demand, too. HERE'S THE 3-STEP FORMULA THAT HAS MADE US MANY MILLIONS OF DOLLARS IN THE PAST: **1.** Find a lucrative market, first (a market is simply a group of people who have something in common that causes them to buy a certain type of product or service). **2.** Then find products and services that are already selling to this established market. **3.** Then find of develop your product or service that are similar to the items that are already selling very well. This is the secret we used to develop our

'Millionaire Training Package'. You must follow this formula to develop your own super valuable product or service.

E) **It must have a high profit margin, so you're able to pay big commissions to your Affiliates while keeping enough profit for yourself.** Although the prices your Affiliates charge to the end customer must be low enough to be attractive, your profit margin must be high enough to pay your Affiliates the biggest commissions possible while still keeping enough money left over for yourself to cover your own overhead and make a profit. This can be an extremely difficult balancing act, and yet it's vital to your success.

Remember, finding or developing the perfect product or service is the critical key to your success. Because of this, I spent a considerable amount of time going over all of the things you must do to make sure you choose the right item that will make you and your affiliate mailers the largest sum of money. The other four ingredients are built on this foundation and will be covered quickly...

Ingredient #2:

An irresistible offer to sell your product or service.

An irresistible offer is a combination of all the things a prospect will receive when they purchase your product or service. The sales materials your provide to your Affiliate Partners must clearly show your prospect the benefits of what they're receiving and it must make the benefits far outweigh the price you are charging. You want it to be attractive that it's almost impossible for them to not buy. <u>Just having a great product or service is not good enough</u>. You must present it in such a way that the prospect is amazed at how much they're getting for the relatively small amount of money that your Affiliates are asking for in return. Again, to

---

use the example of our 'Millionaire Training Program'; the regular value is so high at almost $5,000.00, that when they discover that they can get this entire package for only $495.00, they'll quickly pull our their credit card and place their order. The irresistible offer you create for the products and services in your Affiliate Mailing Program must be as equally compelling.

Ingredient #3:

Powerful sales materials that your Affiliates can use to sell your product or service.

It may shock you to know that some of the best Direct-Response Marketing Copywriters charge up to $15,000.00 plus a 5% royalty on sales to write a single Direct-Mail package (that consists of a sales letter and an order form, and maybe a lift piece or two). The reason they can command such a huge fee is because the Direct-Mail package they charge $15,000.00 to produce could make you millions of dollars in no time flat! For example; we have hired veteran copywriters who have brought us millions of dollars from just one sales letter they wrote for us.

It's no accident that the most successful Direct-Response Marketers have usually been in the business for an average of over 10 years. Why is this? Because it usually takes many years to learn how to develop offers and write sales materials that persuade the largest number of people that what they're offering is more valuable than the money they're asking for.

If you can't afford to hire a seasoned copywriter to produce your Direct-Mail Package for your Affiliates, then you should at least hire one to look over what you have written yourself to add their own suggestions. The money you spend to hire a seasoned veteran to write or rewrite your sales materials could make you many, many thousands of dollars. This is a great investment toward future profits, and can help your Affiliates make the biggest commissions. Don't be too proud to hire a professional copywriter to either write or re-write your sales material. Although we have made millions of dollars in Direct-Mail, it took us many years before we were able to produce our own sales materials without the assistance of veteran copywriters who knew how to write powerful sales materials for us. You should consider doing this yourself.

Ingredient #4:

The best targeted mailing lists money can buy.

Having the best sales materials in the world with the most irresistible offer that sells the most valuable product will still make you no money if you are mailing it to the wrong people. You must provide your Affiliate Mailing Partners with the best mailing lists available.

There are many different mailing lists available, but choosing the right ones is crucial to your success. For example, the mailing lists that we provide to our Affiliate Mailing Partners contain the names and addresses of people who have recently purchased the same types of products and services that are sold in our 'Millionaire Training Package.' You must work with a professional mailing list broker to find the best mailing lists available that contain names and addresses of people who have purchased products and services similar to the ones your Affiliates are selling.

Ingredient #5:

The highest quality Affiliate Support Services you can provide to your Affiliate Partners.

You must take good care of your Affiliate Mailing Partners, and do everything possible to help them make the largest amount of money possible. Because your affiliates are independent contractors, they must be able to promote your products and services in any legal, moral, and ethical manner they choose. However, you can't depend on your affiliates to figure things out on their own. You must provide your affiliates partners with the best sales materials that they can use that will give them the best chance to make the most money. This is especially important if your affiliate partners lack marketing experience. Those affiliates with no marketing experience will tend to use too many of their own ideas and probably fail.

Also, you must introduce your affiliates to the best expert suppliers you can find who can help them in the greatest way. Again, for the sake of an example; we introduce all of our Affiliate Partners to the same expert suppliers that we have used to generate over $100-Million Dollars in Direct-Response Marketing sales. Although our Affiliates are free to do whatever marketing they want to do, we strongly encourage them to use the same expert suppliers we have used to make our fortune. You must do this, too, if you want your Affiliate Partners to succeed in the greatest way.

In Closing...

As you can see, these 5 key ingredients are easy to understand. However, they must be done correctly for you and your Affiliate Partners to be in the position to make the most money.

That brings us to the end of this short book. We hope you enjoyed reading this and have benefited from the ideas we have shared with you. You probably had many doubts when you started reading this book, but by now you (hopefully) know that this really is a rock-solid way to make huge sums of money in the booming Direct-Mail industry.

So with that in mind; please get started today. You can use the information in this Chapter to create your own Affiliate Mailing Program, or you can go to our Web-Site and become one of our

Affiliate Partners, to better acquaint yourself with this powerful way to make huge sums of money.

In closing, I want to thank you again for purchasing this book. I hope to meet you some day at one of our Seminars or Workshops, and have you tell us how this book helped you make a tremendous amount of money.